Smith: A Novel Based On the Play by W. Somerset Maugham

William Somerset Maugham, David Gray

Nabu Public Domain Reprints:

You are holding a reproduction of an original work published before 1923 that is in the public domain in the United States of America, and possibly other countries. You may freely copy and distribute this work as no entity (individual or corporate) has a copyright on the body of the work. This book may contain prior copyright references, and library stamps (as most of these works were scanned from library copies). These have been scanned and retained as part of the historical artifact.

This book may have occasional imperfections such as missing or blurred pages, poor pictures, errant marks, etc. that were either part of the original artifact, or were introduced by the scanning process. We believe this work is culturally important, and despite the imperfections, have elected to bring it back into print as part of our continuing commitment to the preservation of printed works worldwide. We appreciate your understanding of the imperfections in the preservation process, and hope you enjoy this valuable book.

SMITH

"Good Lord," he exclaimed, "I didn't know you had such hair."

SMITH

*A Novel Based on the Play
By W. Somerset Maugham*

BY

DAVID GRAY

NEW YORK
DUFFIELD & COMPANY
1911

Contents

	PAGE
Chapter I Tom Freeman Comes Home	1
Chapter II Rose and Her Friends	9
Chapter III A Sister's Welcome	31
Chapter IV Freeman Declares His Quest	53
Chapter V The Personal "Smith" is Detected	71
Chapter VI Freeman Essays Conversation	87
Chapter VII The Brothers-in-Law Differ	107
Chapter VIII Emily Discloses Her Intentions	129
Chapter IX The Trap is Sprung	145
Chapter X How a Rubber at Bridge was Interrupted	161
Chapter XI Emily Shows Herself in a New Light	185
Chapter XII Freeman is a Second Time Rejected	205

CONTENTS

Chapter XIII
Smith and Freeman Continue Discussion . . . 235

Chapter XIV
Emily Makes New Plans 249

Chapter XV
The Storm Breaks in Credinton Court . . . 271

Chapter XVI
Mr. Peppercorn Makes an Announcement . . 283

Chapter XVII
Tom Freeman Tries Again 297

List of Illustrations

	PAGE
"Good Lord," he exclaimed, "I didn't know you had such hair"	Frontispiece
"Smith received this information in silence"	94
"Oh, no, Ma'am," said Smith; please go at once"	179
"I'm afraid you'll strain yourself, sir," she said politely	260

TOM FREEMAN COMES HOME

SMITH

CHAPTER I

TOM FREEMAN COMES HOME

THE ship came to anchor in the night. With the first light he was standing by the rail gazing at the white cliffs. A barefooted sailor came by with a swab and bucket. "There isn't any mistake about it, is there?" he asked. "It's England?"

"Mistake?" echoed the sailor contemptuously. "'Ow could there be a mistake?" He passed on along the deck and the bronzed, broad-shouldered man in tweeds smiled, turned to the rail again and the grey, misty prospect of Southhampton harbour.

After breakfast, which no one ate, and interminable hours of waiting, the tender finally came off and the sun-browned man stationed by a pile of luggage marked T. F.

waited impatiently for the disbarking. As they neared the shore a little, fitful breeze off the downs brought smells of wet earth and growing things, of England in April, and he filled his lungs rapturously.

In the train shed the porters were running to and fro. The London train was at last about to start. The man that Freeman had sat next to at table all through the voyage from the Cape, brushed by. Freeman held out his hand. "Well," he said, "we're home."

"We've come a long road," said the other man, "but now we're home."

"Is there any place like England?" said Freeman. Then he turned and got into the railway carriage.

As they burst into the country the hedgerows were white with blossom, the meadows were tender green, the roses on the thatched cottage were coming into bloom and Freeman sat by the window of the speeding train and devoured it all with hungry eyes. Early in the afternoon a shower of warm rain broke and passed. The sun came out, the larks fluttered up from the meadows, and through the roar of the train he seemed to hear their twinkling little songs against the country stillness and peace with the subtle inner ear of the heart. It seemed worth the lonely years on the Rhodesian veldt to find it all unchanged, so green, so satisfying to sun-weary eyes, so truly home. As they drew near to London, as the brick-built towns became closer together and they entered the smoky pall of the city, he found that he loved that, too. It, too, was part of home. He caught the name of a station as they flashed by and it told him that they were coming into Waterloo. Again he collected his things, as he had done a half dozen times in the last half hour, and set himself to endure the remaining minutes. But his composure was outward only, for the best of it all was just ahead. There in the great station, only half a mile away, Rose, his sister, was waiting for him; Rose, and very probably her husband, whom he had never seen. He wondered what the unknown brother-in-law would look like. He wondered how the years had dealt with Rose. But after all, that mattered very little. Out of all the world they were the persons that belonged to him. It was them chiefly that made the difference between Rhodesia and England. They were the heart of that curious, intangible, precious thing that we call home, the centre that continuously draws us back across lands and seas to what is ours. It flashed across him half humorously that he was growing unconsciously sentimental, but he did not care. And then the train stopped.

A porter took his luggage and he hurried toward the crowd that was waiting to greet the arriving passengers. A pretty woman waved her hand and he waved back. Then he saw that it was not Rose and that she was waving to someone else. "She must be farther back in the crowd," he thought, and he pressed on, but as the crowd melted he saw that, for the moment, he had missed her.

He walked forward and back, he searched the station with his eyes, but it was apparent that she was not there. For a moment his heart sank. Could anything have happened? was she sick? However, he was not the man to be the prey of forebodings. He decided that she must have been late in starting and he waited longer. Then it suggested itself that perhaps she was down with a headache or a cold and had sent Herbert, her husband. He began to look about for bald-headed men about forty-five, with the appearance of being prosperous barristers, but there was no one to answer the description.

"Anyhow," he muttered, "what difference does it make! They probably didn't get my wire." He turned to the porter. "We won't wait," he said; and the porter asked him if he would have a taxi.

"Taxi?" he repeated. These things had come in the eight years that he had been out of the world. "No," he answered savagely, "put me into a growler." As the door of the old four-wheeler closed with a snap he breathed the musty smell of the damp upholstery and smiled again and they began to thread their way toward Kensington and the adventure that had brought him over ten thousand miles of sea.

ROSE AND HER FRIENDS

CHAPTER II

ROSE AND HER FRIENDS

IT was ten minutes to five when Freeman's train reached Waterloo station. At ten minutes to five in Mrs. Dallas-Baker's drawing-room at Credinton Court, Kensington, there were four people playing bridge, three women and a young man. They played on until presently a little French clock on the mantelshelf began to strike. The young man and Mrs. Dallas-Baker both looked up.

"I say, Rose," said he, "what about tea?"

"Ring the bell," said Mrs. Dallas-Baker.

Mr. Algernon Peppercorn arose, rang the bell and presently a parlour maid appeared.

"Bring the tea," said Mrs. Dallas-Baker. She played a card and then looking up called to the maid: "Is Mr. Freeman's room ready?"

As she spoke the name "Freeman" the

woman who was playing at her left looked quickly up, caught her eye and looked down at her cards again. It was Emily Chapman. She was a woman a little past thirty, who had evidently been handsome, as a girl. But her beauty had faded and it was somewhat obvious that art had been called upon to take its place. She had the look of a woman who had been through hard places without having reaped any spiritual advantages from her experience.

The other woman, Mrs. Otto Rosenberg, a pretty but fading blonde, missed the interchange of glances between Rose and Emily. "Who on earth is Mr. Freeman?" she asked curiously.

"Tom," explained Mr. Peppercorn,—"her brother, her long-lost brother."

Mrs. Rosenberg looked at Rose for confirmation, and Rose nodded. "Yes," she said, "he's coming back to-day." She glanced again at Emily, and Emily again dropped her eyes.

"We can't play bridge, if you talk all the time, can we?" said Emily sharply.

"But aren't you awfully excited?" said Mrs. Rosenberg, still talking to Rose.

"Do I look it?" answered Rose laughing.

Mrs. Rosenberg looked at her doubtfully. "Well," she said, "I suppose we had better stop and settle up."

"Why?" demanded Rose. "Can't we go on after tea?"

"But you will want to get rid of us," Mrs. Rosenberg answered.

"Get rid of you?" Rose repeated in a tone of perplexity.

"But isn't your brother expected soon?" Mrs. Rosenberg explained.

"I think so," answered Rose. "Didn't he wire, Algy, that he was coming about five?"

"His wire said that he was arriving at Waterloo at four-fifty," Mr. Peppercorn replied.

He got up, went to the writing table and

picked up a telegram. "Yes," he went on, "I was quite correct in my statement. It *is* four-fifty."

"But it's past that time now," said Mrs. Rosenberg to Rose. "Didn't you intend to meet him?"

Rose laughed drily. "Good heavens, no!" she answered. "Why on earth should I stand about a draughty station for half an hour?"

"But you haven't seen him for ten years," said Mrs. Rosenberg.

"Eight, to be precise," Rose answered; "but even if it were ten, what is half an hour more or less?"

"When Otto goes to Paris on business for a week," said Mrs. Rosenberg, "I always meet him at the station."

Mr. Peppercorn observed her with polite surprise. "Really?" he remarked. "But doesn't it bore you?"

"Yes, but Otto seems to think I ought to," she answered.

Miss Chapman, who had risen from the

table, turned idly to the fire. "Germans are so sentimental," she said, yawning.

"I wish you wouldn't call him a German," said Mrs. Rosenberg. "He's been naturalised ten years."

"Well," said Rose, also leaving the table, "as regards meeting people, it's just a matter of common sense. I'm sure Tom would hate me to go to meet him just as much as I should hate going. What good would it do either of us?" No one refuted her, and she went on. "I think, Algy, that you're going rather to like him. He's really rather funny, sometimes."

"I dare say I shall like him," Mr. Peppercorn replied vaguely.—"If he doesn't bore me. I forget, what has he been doing out there?"

"Oh, all sorts of things," Rose explained. "I know very little about him, you know. He has written to me once or twice a year, but you see I'm always so busy I never seem to have time to write. I do try to send him a picture post card for Christmas, but that's a great bore. I believe of late he's been farming in Rhodesia."

As Rose talked on she kept an eye on Emily and noted that she was growing uneasy as the minutes passed.

"That sounds a cheerful occupation," observed Mr. Peppercorn, "but I'm quite as well pleased not to be indulging in it. Odd sort of chap that likes to farm."

Before he finished, Emily had begun to move restlessly about the room as if searching for something that was not there. "Haven't you got a mirror glass in here?" she asked at last; "I want to arrange my hat."

"No," said Rose. "We had one, but Algy insisted on our taking it out. I forget why. Why was it, Algy?"

"Because," said Mr. Peppercorn authoritatively, "I hate looking-glasses in drawing-rooms. It's so beastly suburban."

The ladies looked at him submissively and then Emily Chapman turned to Rose. "Do you mind if I go to your room?" she asked.

"It harasses me to think that my hat is on crooked."

"It's quite straight, dear," said Rose, sending her a teasing look, "but go by all means if you're anxious about it. You know the way, don't you?"

"Thank you," said Emily, and she left the room.

Mr. Peppercorn, standing with his back to the fire, teacup in hand, silently watched her departure. When he was certain the door had closed behind her, he looked about him and remarked, "I think she's rather overdone it, to-day, don't you?"

"I hope to goodness," said Rose, "that she's not going to put any more on. Her eyes are too dreadful, now."

"It's a pity," said Mrs. Rosenberg; "why should she make up so?"

Rose smiled knowingly. "She began it," she answered, "after her last engagement was broken off as an outward and visible sign of a broken heart."

Mrs. Rosenberg laughed and Mr. Peppercorn smiled approvingly. "I feel," he observed, "that the psychological moment is arriving when her hair will turn scarlet."

"That's left for her next matrimonial mishap," said Rose.

"She has been dreadfully unlucky, poor thing," observed Mrs. Rosenberg cheerfully.

"Very," said Rose; "but the odd thing, of course, is her being here to-day. You know," she added in response to the general look of inquiry, "that she was engaged to Tom, don't you?"

"No," exclaimed Mrs. Rosenberg. Mr. Peppercorn also deigned to manifest surprise and placed his teacup on the mantelpiece behind him. Then with both hands free to put in his trousers pockets he addressed himself to listen.

"I think," continued Rose, "that Tom was her first, or nearly that. She gave me such an odd look when I first mentioned his name that you would have thought she still cared for him. Perhaps she is thinking that he'll do, after all."

"Did she break it off?" asked Mrs. Rosenberg.

"Yes," said Rose, "but I've never laid it up against her. It was the time when Tom was hammered on the stock exchange and when she found that he was flat broke she very wisely sent him about his business."

"Modern love," observed Mr. Peppercorn thoughtfully, "has a very delicate constitution. It can hardly be expected to withstand a shock like that."

"Well, she *has* had bad luck," continued Rose sympathetically. "After Tom had cut for South Africa, she consoled herself by getting engaged to a man in the army and then what do you think happened?"

"I don't think I ever heard," said Mrs. Rosenberg.

"After they had been engaged for ever and ever, two or three years, at least, the poor fellow was killed somehow or other. Can you imagine a worse bore for her?" She paused a moment to offer more tea to her guests.—"And I believe," she continued, "the worst of it was that he was quite well off. Wasn't it a pity, and of course he never had made a will, so he left her nothing."

"And was it after that she began to rouge?" inquired Mr. Peppercorn.

"Oh no," said Rose; "she only powdered after that." She stopped a moment in thought, while her audience waited attentively. "She didn't rouge," Rose went on, "until after the Einstein match was broken off. That *was* hard luck, you know."

"A little more cake for Algy," said Mr. Peppercorn, "and then continue, please, with the details of this deplorable affair. I don't remember ever to have heard them and one should show some interest in the lives of one's friends."

"Well," said Rose, "it was positively a tragedy. Just before the marriage he was made the co-respondent in a divorce case and when it was all over he went to Emily and said that as he'd ruined the woman, you see, and as she'd lost her position and heaven knows what, he felt it his duty to marry her."

"I say that was a bit rough on Emily!" exclaimed Mr. Peppercorn with his mouth full of cake.

"I think it was *very* rough," said Rose, "for she's thirty-two, if she's a day. My impression is that she'd accept a chimney sweep if he asked her."

"Well, I suppose you probably know," said Mrs. Rosenberg. "She is a great friend of yours, isn't she?"

"Oh, yes," replied Rose, "I'm devoted to her. I've never let the manner in which she treated Tom influence me in the least, and I've always defended her whenever people have talked, as I am sorry to say they sometimes have done. Of course," Rose continued, "there are some things which people say, which one simply can't deny. We all know she hasn't a farthing, yet look at the way she dresses."

"Personally," observed Mr. Peppercorn, "I think she plays bridge a bit *too* well."

Rose nodded. "I only ask her," she said, "when I can't get anybody to make a fourth. I know that she always wins, and I find it quite hard enough to pay for my own frocks without helping to pay for hers."

"She really dresses very nicely," said Mrs. Rosenberg, not without a touch of envy in her tone.

"She does," said Rose, "and I often wonder if it's only on bridge that she does it."

"At all events," said Mr. Peppercorn, "let us believe the worst about her. I think I hear her coming down the passage." They were silent for a moment listening and then the door opened and Miss Chapman came in again. She glanced shrewdly around the room and smiled. "Well," she said, "have you been tearing my character to pieces?"

Mr. Peppercorn looked at her admiringly and went to the tea-tray with his empty cup. "Darling," he said, "we haven't left you a shred, but I have generously left you nearly half of the plum cake and you may have some tea."

"I felt that I must choose between my hat and my character when I went out," said Miss Chapman, helping herself to the proffered cake.

"And," said Rose cheerfully, "you wisely chose the more important." She broke off as the door opened again. "Ah, here comes my lord and master," she observed, "instead of brother Tom." She nodded to a stout, smooth-shaven man, about forty-five, who stood in the doorway.

Herbert Dallas-Baker was a very bald, easy-going, pompous and rather commonplace type of barrister, extremely well satisfied to be a K. C. "How d'you do?" he said pleasantly enough and shook hands with Mrs. Rosenberg and Emily. To Mr. Peppercorn he merely said, "Hulloa, Algy," whereupon Mr. Peppercorn very simply turned his back and went to the window and closed it. On his return to the fireplace he acknowledged the salutation by saying, "Hulloa!"

"You've just come in time for tea," observed Rose. "Rather early for you, isn't it?"

"There was nothing doing in Chambers," said Dallas-Baker, "so I thought I'd drop in and see if there was any bridge."

"You must take my place," said Mrs. Rosenberg; "I must be going."

"Not at all," said Rose firmly. "We shall cut out."

"I suppose," said Mr. Dallas-Baker, after being supplied with tea, "that your brother hasn't turned up yet."

"No," said Rose, "I dare say his train is late or something. Algy said he ought to have arrived at Waterloo at ten minutes before five."

"Oh, I dare say he'll get here," said Dallas-Baker hopefully. "It's rather funny," he went on to Mrs. Rosenberg, "I've never seen him, you know. I didn't meet Rose till after he had gone out to the Cape."

"Well, I've half a mind to think you'll like him," said Rose. "He's one of those restful people who take nothing seriously. He has no morals and no conscience."

"He sounds perfectly delightful!" observed Mrs. Rosenberg.

"And on the other hand," Rose continued, "he has a very neat gift for repartee and a really keen sense of humour."

"Which is much more useful in a wicked world," observed Mr. Peppercorn profoundly. As he uttered this oracle he went to the card table and began a game of solitaire.

"Still, he may have changed in eight years," suggested Miss Chapman, who had been listening in silence.

Rose shook her head and gave Emily a quizzical look. "No," she said, "I'm sure that he will be the same flippant, careless, delicious creature that he always was. Rather like Algy, don't you think?"

Miss Chapman looked at Mr. Peppercorn. "No," she said decidedly and with a slight curling of the nostril,—"not in the least."

"I thank you," said Mr. Peppercorn gently, as he dealt the cards.

"Well, of course, I dare say I have forgotten him," said Rose tolerantly. "So many things happen in eight years to blot out old impressions. Except for the sentiment of it, we're really quite strangers, aren't we? And sentiment, after all, is such rot."

Dallas-Baker evidently was not interested in these speculative questions, for he turned to Mr. Peppercorn. "What have you been doing to-day, Algy?" he inquired.

Mr. Peppercorn waited until he had pondered his next play and made it, then he turned pleasantly to his host. "Oh, we've had rather a busy day," he answered, "haven't we, Rose?"

"We have, rather," assented Rose.

"To begin with," continued Mr. Peppercorn, "I rolled up about eleven and took Rose to have a frock tried on."

"Herbert," said Rose to her husband, "you can't imagine how invaluable Algy is at the dressmaker's. He is so full of ingenious ideas."

"If I may say it without vanity," observed Mr. Peppercorn, for the moment suspending his solitaire, "I do know a thing or two about frocks. But why shouldn't I?"

Mrs. Rosenberg laughed. "I wonder what Otto would say," she observed, "if I took a young man to help me try on a new gown?"

Dallas-Baker glanced from Mrs. Rosenberg to his wife. "I suppose it would depend upon the result," he observed quietly.

"I think Otto sounds rather suburban," said Rose firmly.

"He's not exactly suburban," said Mrs. Rosenberg defensively. "He's Maida Vale."

"Be that as it may," said Algy, continuing his chronicle of the day. "After the dressmaker's we came back here and lunched and we've played bridge ever since. Rather a hard day, what?"

Dallas-Baker said nothing, but helped himself to bread and butter.

"I do think London is very tiring!" said Rose.

Miss Chapman went to the card table and seated herself opposite Mr. Peppercorn. "If we want another rubber before dinner," she said, "we ought not to waste any more time."

Mrs. Rosenberg rose as if about to go. "I'm not going to play any more," she said to Dallas-Baker. "I'm afraid I haven't time for another rubber; you must take my place."

"You're sure I'm not driving you away?" he asked. "We wish you'd stop on." As her tone seemed really to mean that she was going, his polite insistence that she remain was quite warm and genuine.

"No, I really can't play any more," she replied. "I'll just wait a minute and see what the hands are and then I'll fly."

"Come, then," said Miss Chapman, "let's cut for partners."

The cards made Emily and Dallas-Baker

play together, with Rose and Mr. Peppercorn against them.

"Are you weak and weak?" asked Dallas-Baker of his partner.

"I am," said Emily.

"So am I," said Dallas-Baker.

"You don't mind light no trumpers, do you?" Miss Chapman asked.

"No," he agreed again.

"It's the only way to make money," she said decidedly.

"You put the fear of God into me, Miss Chapman," said Mr. Peppercorn reverently; and with this interesting and intellectual prelude the rubber began.

Rose gathered up her hand, glanced through it and smiled. There was a blush of red cards, all the honours in hearts, certain outside aces and a long suit in clubs. Suddenly a disturbing thought flashed upon her. "I say," she remarked ruefully, "it will be an awful bore if Tom comes before we have finished the rubber."

"A merciful Providence," observed Mr. Peppercorn hopefully, "is always good to card players."

"Well, I'll tell you now," said Rose firmly, "nothing will induce me to stop in the middle of a hand whether it is good or bad." No one said anything. "I'm going to make this hearts," she added.

"Probably," said Dallas-Baker smiling, "she's got 'em all."

"I hope so," said Mr. Peppercorn.

"Shall I play to hearts, partner?" asked Miss Chapman.

"Please do," said Dallas-Baker. Miss Chapman led her card, Mr. Peppercorn laid down his hand as dummy and then the door opened and the maid announced, "Mr. Freeman!"

A SISTER'S WELCOME

CHAPTER III

A SISTER'S WELCOME

As the newcomer was announced, the bridge players turned and saw the sun-tanned, broad-shouldered young man that had left the train half an hour before at Waterloo, standing in the doorway with his hat and coat on, and a travelling rug over his arm. He looked about him for a moment in perplexity, searching for his sister. Then he burst in with a hearty, rather boyish laugh and a boy's enthusiasm and eagerness of manner. "Rose! Rose! Rose!" he called.

Rose gathered up her cards with a gesture of vexation and turned to him. "Tactless creature!" she said. "You might have waited till I was dummy!"

Tom Freeman stopped and looked at her in amazement.

"Don't you understand," she went on, "that I had just begun the hand? It will only take a few minutes. You do understand, don't you?" She turned back to the table and leaned over to inspect the dummy's cards that Mr. Peppercorn had laid down. "Let me see what you've given me," she said.

Freeman stood in dumbfounded silence at her side still wearing his hat and coat, when suddenly the low, pleasant voice of the maid sounded in his ear. "Shall I take your coat and things, sir?" she asked.

"If you wouldn't mind," he answered.

She helped him off with the coat and took it and the rug and then his hat, all so quietly and swiftly that he turned and glanced after her. As she turned back in the passageway to close the door, he noticed that she was very good to look at. Even with her straw-coloured hair done tightly under her maid's cap, he could see that it was quite extraordinary hair, and her fresh English pink-and-white skin and the violet of her eyes and her strong, young, flat-backed figure wore no disguise. There were no pictures like that

A SISTER'S WELCOME

in Rhodesia and he had not got used to them in England, so he felt excused for staring at her. It was only for a moment, however, that his glance strayed after her, and then he turned to his sister again. He smiled grimly at the party at the table, who were watching in more or less embarrassed silence, bent down, took the cards gently from her hand and laid them on the table. Then he lifted her out of her chair and drew her up to him to kiss her. "Rose," he said, "I haven't seen you for eight years; do you realise it?"

"Don't be idiotic on that account," she cried. "Do let me go on, don't you see I've got to play out the hand!"

"Come, give me a kiss," he commanded. She put her hands stubbornly before her face.

"Not till you behave," she replied. "I had no idea," she explained apologetically to the others, "that my brother was going to make a scene."

Dallas-Baker rose and moved about the

card table toward his brother-in-law and Emily Chapman noticing it laid down her cards. "We'd better give the game up," she said, "don't you think so?"

"I suppose we'll have to," exclaimed Rose gracelessly. *"You're* willing enough," she went on, "because you probably had a rotten hand, but I had a very good one and I don't see why Tom couldn't have waited five minutes till I'd played it. We could have been just as affectionate five minutes later."

"Don't talk so much," said Freeman, drawing her closer to him, "and give me a kiss."

"You're like a bull in a china shop," she answered, but she smiled at him rather sulkily and kissed him.

"There, that's better," he said. "You know I was frightened out of my wits when I got to Waterloo. I was afraid you were ill, or worse, when I didn't see you at the station."

"But you didn't expect me to go all the

way to that awful station and meet you?" Rose answered.

"I did, indeed, selfish little beast," he said gaily. He looked at her affectionately and kissed her again. "But it doesn't matter," he went on with a laugh, "I've got you now and I'm not going to let you go. By George, I am glad to see you again!"

"You are making everybody feel very uncomfortable," said Rose unresignedly, "and me perfectly absurd."

"Then I apologise," said Freeman, and let her go.

Rose smoothed her ruffled plumage and withdrew out of reach. "If I had known that he was going to behave in this way," she said to the company in general, "I should have received him in strict privacy."

Freeman laughed and cast his eye questioningly from one to the other of the two men, both of whom were strangers to him. Then he turned to Peppercorn and held out his hand. "I suppose you are my brother-in-law," he said.

"I am delighted to shake hands with you," replied Mr. Peppercorn, "but I haven't the honour of the relationship that you suggest."

"This is Herbert," said Rose, and Dallas-Baker came forward, chuckling at the mistake that Freeman had made.

"You might have sent me a photograph," said Freeman with some embarrassment.

"I find," replied Dallas-Baker, "that when one grows bald the camera has no great attraction for one."

"I suppose that is so," Freeman assented. As he released his brother-in-law's hand, his eyes fell upon Emily Chapman, whom he had not noticed before.

"You remember Emily," said Rose with a slight smile.

Freeman's enthusiastic manner returned at once. "By Jove, it is Emily!" he exclaimed, "and it is ripping to see you. You haven't changed a bit!" He took both her hands and shook them violently.

"It is nice of you to say so," said Emily.

"And this is Cynthia," Rose went on with a look at Mrs. Rosenberg. "You remember Cynthia Russell?"

For a moment he was at a loss. Then he burst into one of his hearty, infectious laughs. "But Cynthia was a kid when I left," he cried. He held out his hand. "Good gracious, how old I'm growing. Your baldness, Herbert, is nothing to it!"

"I'm afraid it's how do you do, and goodbye," said Mrs. Rosenberg. "I really must be going. I think my husband used to know you when you were on the stock exchange."

"You don't mean to say that you are married!" Freeman exclaimed with gallant surprise. "What is his name?"

"Otto Rosenberg," she answered.

"No," he said thoughtfully, "I don't think I ever knew him. I used to know a fat old German called Rosenberg, but he was old enough to be your father." He looked up and caught Rose's eye signalling disapproval, and the next moment Mrs. Rosenberg laughed.

"That is my husband," she said.

Freeman looked at her aghast. "Oh, I beg your pardon," he said clumsily. "I am so sorry."

"It doesn't matter at all," said Mrs. Rosenberg amicably. "People do call him a fat old German, but there is not a girl I know who wouldn't have been glad to marry him."

"As long as you are happy, that is the chief thing, isn't it?" said Freeman, and he gave her one of his hearty, good-natured smiles.

She nodded. "Yes, indeed," she said.

"By the way," observed Mr. Peppercorn, as if he had forgotten something, "how is your son and heir to-day? I had forgotten to enquire."

"He was rather seedy this morning," replied Mrs. Rosenberg, "and very cross, I fear. But I don't really know, for I just saw him for two minutes before I went out."

Freeman listened interestedly. "Have

A SISTER'S WELCOME

you really got a baby?" he asked. "How old is he?"

Mrs. Rosenberg was looking at the watch hanging from the jewelled pin on her blouse when he spoke and she answered rather absently, "Six weeks. Good heavens!" she exclaimed. "I had no idea how late it was. I have only just got time to get back and dress for the opera. Otto's so funny, he hates arriving late."

"But are you able to leave your baby all day?" Freeman inquired.

Mrs. Rosenberg looked from Rose to the questioner in mild amazement. "He's got a nurse," she said.

Freeman looked somewhat at a loss. "I beg your pardon," he said and laughed drily. "In Rhodesia we're rather primitive in our habits."

Mrs. Rosenberg laughed, too. "You're forgiven," she said. "What absurd creatures you must be in Africa! Good-bye, dear," she called to Rose, "I *have* enjoyed my afternoon." Rose returned her salutation. The two women kissed amicably and Mrs. Rosenberg left the room. As soon as she was well out of hearing, Rose turned to her brother and burst into a fit of laughing. "What ever made you say that to Cynthia?" she exclaimed.

"Say what?" demanded Freeman.

"About leaving her baby," Rose replied.

"Well," said Freeman, "why shouldn't I? I think women ought to look after their babies if they're lucky enough to have them."

Rose was about to reply, but she checked herself as the maid who had taken Freeman's coat and hat entered the room and approached him. "Would you give me the key of your box, sir?" she said in a low, pleasant voice. "I've unpacked the dressing-case."

"Thank you very much," he said. He gave her the keys and followed her with his eyes again as she turned and left the room. "It's rather nice to have someone to do things for you, when you've had to do everything for yourself for the Lord knows how long," he observed to Dallas-Baker. "You people don't appreciate it. By the way," he added, "what's the name of that parlour maid, Rose?"

"Smith," was the reply.

"Smith?" Freeman repeated, "that all! what goes first?"

Rose looked at him scornfully. "How should I know?" she demanded.

"I don't know," he answered, "but I should think you would, that's all."

"Isn't she something new?" asked Emily Chapman.

"No," said Rose, "I've had her since last summer."

"Really," said Emily in mild surprise. "I somehow had never noticed her before. But I never do know my friends' servants apart. It's stupid of me!"

Freeman said nothing, but it seemed to him that it was stupid.

"I got her in the country," Rose continued. "Her father has a farm near the house we took for the long vacation. We used to get our eggs and butter there. She wanted a place, so I took her."

"Hadn't she been in service before?" Emily asked idly.

"Oh, yes," said Rose. "She's been in some very good houses, but only in the country. She was anxious to come to London."

"She's the best maid we've had for a long time," Dallas-Baker volunteered.

"She *has* been rather a success," said Rose. "She works like a horse and she's a very good needlewoman."

"And her manners are so good," said Dallas-Baker again.

"She's a handsome woman," said Freeman quietly.

"A parlour maid," said Rose, correcting him, "isn't 'a handsome woman'; she has a 'good appearance.'" There was a laugh at this and she went on. "That's really why I engaged her. Algy hates me to have ugly maids."

"Does anyone blame me?" asked Mr. Peppercorn.

Emily Chapman rose at this point. "I think I am going to leave you to enjoy one another's society," she said. "I feel sure that you want to fall on one another's necks and talk about long deceased relatives."

"No, we don't," said Rose earnestly. "Please don't go."

"I must," said Miss Chapman decisively. "I have had a very nice afternoon."

"I'm sorry our bridge was interrupted," Rose observed stiffly.

"I'm not," said Miss Chapman with a smile. She held out her hand to Freeman simply and frankly. "Good-bye," she said.

"Good-bye," he answered. He took both her hands and held them a moment. "I'm so glad to have seen you again. I hope to see a lot of you while I'm here."

She dropped her eyes, apparently somewhat embarrassed. "I'm surprised that you haven't forgotten me," she said, colouring.

"What nonsense!" he exclaimed. "I've often wondered what had become of you,

Emily. It does one good to see old friends, when one has been away as long as I have."

She looked gratefully at him, withdrew her hands and saying "good-bye" to the room in general, opened the door and left.

Freeman watched her until she had gone and then sat down. "Nice girl," he said to his sister. "I'm sorry she hasn't married. It would have been a good thing for her to marry."

Rose lifted her eyebrows. "Didn't it make you a little uncomfortable," she asked, "to see her again?"

"And why?" demanded Freeman.

"You haven't forgotten that you were engaged to her," said Rose bluntly.

"That's no reason why we shouldn't be friends now, is it?" he retorted.

Rose laughed sneeringly. "No," she said. "After all, she only threw you over because you went broke."

"Well, I bear her no ill-will for that," Freeman answered. "I dare say it was very natural." There was a pause and Mr. Peppercorn, who had been sitting in silence, playing solitaire at the card table, looked up from his game with a judicial and patronising manner.

"You appear to have a charming nature," he said.

Freeman bit his lip. He was clearly vexed, but he controlled himself. "By the way," he said in a tone of pleasant enquiry, "who are you, anyway?"

"I?" drawled Mr. Peppercorn. "Oh, nobody; just Algy."

"That sufficiently explains itself," said Freeman. "I was hoping for information."

Mr. Peppercorn laughed amiably. "You have a pleasant way of putting things, haven't you?" he said.

"Now, look here," said Freeman. "I don't want to seem disagreeable, but you show no signs of making a move and I haven't seen my sister for eight years. Don't you think it would be a good idea if you hooked it?"

Mr. Peppercorn looked up from his rows of cards with an air of amused tolerance and caught Rose's eye, as much as to say, "Do explain to this creature."

Rose laughed. "Tom," she exclaimed, "you must behave yourself. If you don't yet love Algy, you can't neglect the forms of good society."

"Damn good society," said Freeman, calmly. "I didn't come from Rhodesia to see Algy."

"That is fortunately true," said Mr. Peppercorn, "yet after what has passed it would be difficult to make my departure look quite natural, wouldn't it? So I think I'll have to stay."

Dallas-Baker, who had been escorting Miss Chapman to the door, returned just in time to hear the end of Peppercorn's reply. "Of course you're going to stay to dinner, aren't you?" he said hospitably.

"Well, you see," replied Mr. Peppercorn, "your brother-in-law seems to think that he would like to enjoy the society of his family without—" he hesitated for the word and Freeman supplied it for him—

"An outsider," he said drily.

"Nonsense!" exclaimed Rose, somewhat sharply. "Of course you must stay as usual."

Mr. Peppercorn's indecision vanished at this. He turned to Freeman. "Sorry to annoy," he said cheerfully, "but this is a command, isn't it? Besides, Rose's cook is so much better than mother's, you oughtn't to blame me." He turned to Dallas-Baker: "I'll just go and telephone to mother and tell her to send my clothes along. I can change in your room, can't I, Herbert?"

"Certainly," said Herbert. The master of the house then turned to Freeman, shrugged his shoulders, smiled, and lit a cigarette. "You must be very glad to be home again," he said pleasantly.

"Glad!" exclaimed Freeman ecstatically, "you don't know how often I've lain awake at night out there and longed for the green lanes and jolly grey skies of England."

Mr. Peppercorn, on his way to the telephone, had reached the door at this point in Freeman's rhapsody. He half opened it. "Rose," he called back, "stop him! He's just about to call it a tight little island!" and disappeared.

Freeman bit his lip, but took no notice of the interruption. "And when I landed," he went on, "I could have hugged everyone I saw, man, woman and child. The green trees, the great fat fields, the little red brick villas, all had come true again! I kept saying to myself, 'It's England! England!'"

"Moderate your transports, dear," said Rose, looking up from the writing table, where she had begun to compose a note. "You are making yourself a little ridiculous, don't you think?"

"What do I care!" he answered vehemently and went on to his brother-in-law: "At Waterloo the porter asked me if I'd have a taxi. 'Not at any price,' I answered. 'Get me a growler.' And when I got in and smelled its good old musty stink, I really felt I was in London."

"You will find a great many changes since you went away," observed Dallas-Baker pompously. "Motor cabs, motor busses, tubes. We've forged ahead since you left us."

Freeman looked thoughtfully at the ceiling. "I wonder," he said slowly.

"Oh, yes," said Dallas-Baker with impressive confidence. "You may take my word for it. The progress of the past ten years has been perfectly phenomenal."

"But is it all progress?" Freeman insisted.

Rose finished her note and pushed her chair back from the writing table. "You are getting prosy, Herbert," she remarked.

"Am I?" he replied. "Still," he continued to Freeman, "it's all progress and it has resulted in the greatest city the world has ever known, prose or no prose. And now," he added, rising, "I'll go and see what wine Smith has got out for dinner," and he left the room.

FREEMAN DECLARES HIS QUEST

CHAPTER IV

FREEMAN DECLARES HIS QUEST

When Freeman and Rose were at last left together, the brother turned to her. She was still at the writing table. "I'm sorry," he said, "that I was rather sniffy with your friend, just now; but I did so want to be alone with you! You can understand it, can't you?"

"You've succeeded in putting your foot into it very thoroughly since you arrived," she replied, without looking up.

"Never mind," he said. "I daresay they'll forgive me, and if they don't, I can't help it. What I want now is to look at you and get acquainted again. He went to the desk and took her hand. She protested, insisting that she wanted to finish her letter and drew her hand away, but he seized her, picked her up from her chair and took her in his arms. She struggled to escape, but he held her firmly. "Don't be idiotic!" she exclaimed at last.

He looked her steadfastly in the eyes for a moment, as if he were trying to read her innermost thoughts. "Are you happy?" he asked.

"Of course I'm happy," she replied.

"I'm glad of that," he said with feeling. "I've been so anxious about you."

"Why?" she demanded. She drew herself away again and he reluctantly released her.

"Well," he said, "in the first place I knew nothing about your husband, except that he was a good deal older than you."

"That's inevitable," Rose answered, "unless you want to scrub along on twopence a year. Men don't seem to earn enough to keep a wife decently until they're about forty."

Freeman sighed and smiled rather mournfully. "Well," he said slowly, "I am so relieved that it's all right."

Rose looked at him curiously. "What on

earth have you been fussing about?" she demanded. "What did you think was wrong?"

"I was afraid," he answered gravely, "that you might be awfully disappointed at having no children."

She burst into a gay laugh. "You're a perfect fool, Tom, dear!" she exclaimed. "Herbert makes about fifteen hundred a year and we have a very decent time on it. We go to San Moritz and Paris and Marienbad, and we take a house in the country. And if we're bored, we can always stand ourselves a theatre and a little supper at the Carlton. But we couldn't do that if we had half a dozen children."

Freeman looked at her without speaking for a moment. Then he said drily, "I see. That never struck me before."

"And besides," Rose went on, "I want to enjoy myself. For six months Cynthia Rosenberg couldn't do anything. She led a dog's life." She broke off as her husband entered the room again.

"I thought we'd kill the fatted calf," he said with his unctuous smile, "and celebrate the prodigal's return."

"That sounds like champagne," suggested Rose.

"Right," said Dallas-Baker. "I've got just a little more Bollinger 1900. I thought this would be an admirable opportunity to drink it."

"That's awfully good of you," said Freeman. "It's a long while since anything with the glory of a vintage label has come my way."

"Well, you see now," said Rose with a smile, "the logic of my philosophy. We couldn't give you vintage Bollinger if we had to provide for a pack of squalling brats."

Freeman laughed good-humouredly. "I would as soon drink beer," he said.

"I wouldn't," said Mr. Peppercorn, who had returned noiselessly. "I consider beer provincial and liverish, as well. My mother," he continued, addressing the room in general, "sends her love by the telephone and my clothes by a messenger boy."

"She is a most well-trained parent," said Rose. "Thank her for us for the love and be grateful yourself for the clothes."

Mr. Peppercorn bowed his acknowledgments and taking a chair from the side of the room with ostentatious gravity, placed it directly in front of the one in which Freeman had seated himself. Then he sat down, crossed his legs and folded his hands. "Now!" he murmured.

Freeman looked at him in half-amused surprise. "What are you doing that for?" he demanded.

"Just before you came," said Mr. Peppercorn, "Rose was assuring us that you had a pretty wit. We have leisure now until it is time to change for dinner. Pray scintillate."

Freeman threw back his head and laughed his boisterous laugh. "You're a foolish youth," he said. "But if I was rude to you just now, I beg your pardon."

"You *were* rude to me," replied Mr. Peppercorn mildly, "but by begging my pardon you assume a pose of superiority which I resent."

Freeman stopped laughing and looked at him in amazement. "I'm afraid I don't understand what you are talking about," he said slowly.

"Then I beg *your* pardon," said Mr. Peppercorn. "In all future conversation I will do my best to confine myself to words of two syllables."

Freeman's look of amazement deepened as the youth went on. Then he began to smile somewhat mirthlessly. "I dimly perceive," he said, "that you are trying to make yourself disagreeable and I wonder why?"

Mr. Peppercorn took his cigarette case from his breast pocket with a somewhat feminine exaggeration in the way he used his hands, opened it and offered it to his vis à vis with profound ceremony. Freeman took one. "I am coming to the conclusion," he said thoughtfully, "that I don't like you."

"It distresses me infinitely," said Freeman. "But may I enquire why?"

"As to that, I haven't quite made up my mind," said Mr. Peppercorn. "I only know that at present you don't quite meet with my approval. You don't mind my telling you, do you?" he added. He struck a match and offered it politely.

"Not at all," said Freeman. He took the match, lighted his cigarette, after which he returned it with equal punctiliousness. "I never mind what a man says to me," he continued, "when I know that I can knock him down if I want to."

Mr. Peppercorn turned to Rose, as if he had been inspecting a zoological specimen in a glass case and was about to report on it. "You know, Rose," he said, "this brother of yours is uncivilised. That is what is the matter with him. He smells so strongly of mother earth."

Rose laughed. "You're simply marvellous at analysis, Algy," she said.

"And I suppose that your nostrils are

more accustomed to patchouli," said Freeman good-naturedly.

"Good!" exclaimed Mr. Peppercorn. "A repartee at last! But what a bad one! You're lamentably of your period, sir!"

"I beg your pardon," said Freeman. "I don't understand."

"You positively reek of nineteen hundred and one," said Mr. Peppercorn, shuddering at the thought,—"a dreadful chapter in our common past which the civilised have left behind them."

"Yes," said Rose, shaking her head, "you are a great disappointment, Tom. I can see already that you've changed in the most extraordinary way."

"I?" exclaimed Freeman indignantly. "I changed? Is it really possible? If you had asked me an hour ago, I should have said that I was the same as ever I had been, but now I am wondering. Perhaps you are right. It is certain that somebody has changed. Is it I or all of you?"

"Oh, my dear!" said Rose, with an air of

comic desperation, "please don't take a casual remark too seriously! What would become of conversation, if every time one said it was a fine day, one was answered with a psychological reflection?" She dropped into an armchair by the fire and began idly arranging the coals with the poker.

"I suppose," said Freeman gravely, "that I really have changed. I remember that I left England with a sinking heart. When the slump came that broke me, I thought that I had lost everything worth living for." He paused and flicked the ashes of his cigarette into the fire. No one spoke and he went on: "I couldn't realise that life was possible away from London, with the theatres and music halls. My idea of a holiday in those days was the river and Maidenhead. My idea of pleasure a supper at Romano's. I hunted a bit, raced a bit, and I have no doubt drank more than was good for me."

"My dear fellow," said Mr. Peppercorn, interrupting him as he finished his sentence, "aren't you making a speech?"

"I suppose," said Freeman, continuing on without apparent regard for the interruption, and scrutinising the immaculate youth soberly, "I suppose that in those days I must have been very like you."

"I beg your pardon!" observed Mr. Peppercorn.

"I said," repeated Freeman, "that I suppose that in those days I must have been very like you. I see in you, Algy, the man I think now that I must have been, and, to be frank, I'm filled with a very lively feeling of disgust."

"I don't believe that you were ever half so agreeable as I am," observed Mr. Peppercorn.

"Yes," said Freeman vaguely, gazing at Rose's operations with the poker, "I bless that slump that ruined me. Except for that, I might be making five thousand pounds a year."

"And Emily Chapman would be driving her own car," suggested Rose softly.

"Yes," he assented, "and I sitting beside her, such a man as our Algy."

Dallas-Baker, who had been reading the evening paper by the lamp, suddenly looked up. "But what on earth made you go out to the Cape?" he asked.

"It was the obvious thing to do," replied Freeman absently, "and I had done the obvious all my life."

"If you had only kept on," suggested Mr. Peppercorn, "you might have been a cabinet minister by now. That's something we've been spared."

Freeman smiled drily. "That makes me think of what I was, too," he observed, "but not long after I got out to the Cape it was borne in upon me that a knack of saying rather funny things was not as useful as a good heavy fist, and within three months I was thanking my stars that I had the fist."

"Why?" said Rose.

"Because," Freeman went on, "when I came to the end of my journey, I was glad to get a job as luggage porter in a Joburg hotel, and I got it because anyone could see that I was a beefy sort of cove."

A shade crosed Rose's face. "But why didn't you write?" she said gently.

"Well," said Freeman, "I thought that I should like to come through on my own. And I've done it. I've got a rattling fine farm in Rhodesia and I've made a bit of money. There is only one thing in the world that I want now, and I've come all the way to England to get it. You've wondered what brought me home, and I'm going to tell you."

"And what is it?" Dallas-Baker asked.

"It's even money," suggested Mr. Peppercorn, "between an agricultural implement and a bagatelle board."

"It happens to be neither," said Freeman.

"Sold again," said Mr. Peppercorn. "I am a bad guesser. We give up!"

"Well," said Rose, "tell us."

Freeman looked meditatively into the coals. "For a good many years," he began,

"I had to work so devilish hard that I had no time for thinking, but after a bit I began to think a little. I used to look at dawn on the edge of the veldt and think how jolly life was; and I used to look at the stars and wonder what the devil life meant. But after a time I got sick of that."

"And I'm sure not one of us would blame you," volunteered Mr. Peppercorn.

"I got sick of all that," repeated Freeman, heedless of the interruption, "and I grew restless and dumpy. I couldn't make out what the deuce was the matter with me for a long while, but suddenly I hit it! I knew what I wanted and I packed my trunk the next day."

"Well," said Rose, "out with it! Suspense is very trying."

"But my dear girl," Freeman replied, "what should it be? I had discovered that man is not made to live alone."

"You are after a wife?" said Rose.

"I have six clear weeks in which to find one," said Freeman.

"Then you had better advertise at once," said Mr. Peppercorn. "That will surely save not only time but trouble."

"Well, I wouldn't mind that at a pinch," said Freeman. "But I thought Rose might be able to do something for me."

"I?" said Rose. "Do you want me to find you a wife?"

"I do," said Freeman.

"Rose," said Mr. Peppercorn, "we'll start a matrimonial agency. I've got thirteen in mind already." He turned over the bridge scoring tablet and began to write a column of names on the back of it. "I'll arrange them alphabetically."

"You must give us the exact list of your requirements," said Rose, laughing.

"I haven't got many," Freeman answered. "I only want my wife to be a decent, honest sort of woman, not afraid of work. It's no good her caring for society, because the only society that she is likely to have for a long time is mine."

Rose and Mr. Peppercorn looked at one

another. "I can't think of anyone," said Rose, "who'd do for that place."

"I can't imagine one," said Mr. Peppercorn.

Just then the door opened and Smith, the parlour maid, entered. "A messenger boy has brought your bag, sir," she said to Mr. Peppercorn. "There's eightpence to pay."

"Oh, Herbert," said Mr. Peppercorn to Dallas-Baker, but without looking round, "I don't seem to have any silver. Would you mind giving Smith eightpence?"

Dallas-Baker produced the eightpence from his trousers pocket. While Smith was waiting for it, she crossed to where Freeman was standing by the fire. "Here are your keys, sir," she said in the low voice that had such a charming quality and intonation.

"Thank you," said Freeman, and he took them from the little silver tray.

Then Smith took the eightpence for the messenger and departed as swiftly and noiselessly as she had come. Freeman watched her go, as he had watched her twice before in the hour that he had spent in his sister's house. She seemed to him a strangely efficient and charming figure against the background of Roses and Algies. And parlour maid or no parlour maid, she was a very beautiful woman. He noticed that she even had long, slender, well-shaped hands. His reflections on the shapeliness of the parlour maid's hands were, however, interrupted by his sister.

"So you want a wife?" Rose said musingly.

"That's what I have told you," he answered simply.

She was silent for a moment. Then she asked with a faint smile: "Do you believe that broken engagements can be mended?"

He made no answer, but Mr. Peppercorn, lighting a fresh cigarette, took it upon himself to reply. "In this wonderful age," he said, "they can mend anything. It's first a question of having the cash to pay for it."

Rose laughed. "Algy," she said, "you are the greatest living philosopher."

THE PERSONAL "SMITH" IS DETECTED

CHAPTER V

THE PERSONAL "SMITH" IS DETECTED

THE first three weeks of Tom Freeman's wife-hunting vacation passed uneventfully and without application to the business in hand. He went to the playhouses and the restaurants, he met old friends and picked up some of the threads of his old life, but he seemed to see it all with new eyes, eyes that saw his beloved England with the broad perspective gained from eight years in South Africa, and the old life failed to satisfy him. Curiously enough, there were even times when he actually felt the shadow of homesickness for the Rhodesian veldt and its sincere, simple, elemental existence passing over him. He knew in his heart that if he were to remain in London it could not be in the currents that he had left eight years before, in which he found the Dallas-Bakers and his friends still floundering on his return. In the midst of the pressure and artificiality of that life he actually felt himself lonelier than on the thinly-peopled veldt, and more than ever he felt the need, of which he had spoken half playfully but with perfect truthfulness to Rose and Algy on the evening of his arrival, yet he had made no visible progress toward satisfying it. To be sure, Emily Chapman he had seen often, but then only by chance. She seemed to drop in for lunch and bridge, and Rose had her to dine occasionally, but, as well as he could judge of his own heart, its beating was as calm in her presence as out of it. Moreover, his judgment told him that Emily would never do for Rhodesia. None of the girls in that set seemed to have either the inclination or capacity for taking life seriously. Often when day-dreaming he tried to picture the woman that he was looking for and he realised with a smile that the strong, supple, feminine figure, the pink-and-white skin indicative of perfect health, the little head with its mass of straw-coloured hair, the violet eyes, the gravity, balance and native sweetness of character which composed his goddess, were things which he borrowed from the parlour maid, Smith. "Parlour maid, or no parlour maid," he said to himself, "she is a beautiful woman, and she is a good and useful one. But one can't marry her because she is a parlour maid. I wonder why?"

One showery May forenoon, Freeman walked slowly back from Bond Street to the flat in Crediton Court with the prospect of lunching alone. Herbert usually lunched in Hall and Rose was lunching out. She had told him that she was lunching with Mrs. Parsons-Pratt. Instead of ringing the bell, he let himself in with a key. The latch worked noiselessly and his step in the passage on the heavy rug made no sound. He put away his hat and umbrella and hearing voices coming from the dining-room, walked rather aimlessly down the passage. A portiere hung across the dining-room doorway and as he reached it he stopped, for through the space between the edge of the curtain and the jamb of the doorway, he saw Smith sitting by the window with a pile of mending on a chair beside her, while a rather perky young cockney, whom he recognised as Fletcher, the porter of the flats, was cleaning the windows. He stood a moment peeking through the slit, for Smith made a pleasant picture as she sat there, sewing with swift, graceful movements. He also had a curiosity to play spy and try to catch a glimpse of her when the presence of any of the "master" class was unsuspected. Smith was so thoroughly "trained" as a servant that he never could get hold of anything which indicated what her mental processes as a woman really were.

Fletcher washed and polished his window and presently in a low and very sweet voice Smith began to hum a few bars of the song, "Oh, it's all right in the summer time."

As she stopped, Fletcher spoke his approval. "That's a nice 'un," he said.

She looked up at the clock. "You'll have to get out of here in a minute," she observed calmly. There was neither apology, regret nor ill nature in her tone. It was a placid statement of fact.

"I've just finished," the young porter replied. "I've only got the polishin' to do."

Smith looked up at him. "It's getting near your dinner time," she said, "isn't it?"

Fletcher grinned amiably. "I've been thinking I felt a vacuum this 'alf hour," he rejoined.

"Is that your last window?" asked Smith.

"Yes, and jolly glad I am, too," replied Fletcher. "I've been cleanin' windows since eight o'clock this mornin'. Well," he went on musingly, "it 'as it's reward. I like to get 'em over. When I sits down to my sausage and mash, I like to say to myself, there, Albert, you've earned so much, anyway. That is yours."

"I suppose it pays you pretty well cleaning windows," observed Smith without looking up. She broke off a length of thread and swiftly passed it into the needle's eye.

"Well, it depends what you call payin'," answered Fletcher.

"How much do they give you?" she asked again.

"Sixpence a window," he said, "large and small."

"And what do you do with the money?" she asked.

"Put it in the savin's bank," he answered proudly. "That's one thing people can't say about me. They can't say I'm not steady." He turned to the window with an air of conscious virtue and fell to polishing it vigorously.

Smith glanced up and Freeman saw what he had never seen before in her, a light of real, human mischief in her eyes. "And there is another thing they can't say about you," she observed—"they can't say that you haven't got a good opinion of yourself."

Fletcher left off polishing and turned towards her. "That's a nice thing to say to a fellow," he growled sulkily.

"That's why I said it," rejoined Smith sweetly.

The porter gave the glass a finishing rub, pressed the window down and began to gather up his cloths and pail. "I kep' this room till last," he said enigmatically.

"Convenient for me just when lunch is ready," said Smith with sarcasm.

"I suppose you don't know why, do you?" asked Fletcher.

"I do not," said Smith, with supercilious disingenuousness.

"Well," said Fletcher, "you give a guess and I'll tell you if you are right."

"I've got something better to do, thank you," she replied.

Fletcher set down his pail and ladder, squared off and looked at her determinedly. "Look 'ere," he began, "you ain't forgot wot I asked you the other day?"

"I haven't had much chance," said Smith, "as you've reminded me every time I've seen you."

"Well," said Fletcher, "wot 'ave you got against me?"

At this juncture it occurred to Freeman that he was in the position of a man with his ear at a keyhole, but he did not attempt to withdraw. He had no very great delicacy as regards Mr. Fletcher. As for Smith, something in her manner told him that he was not likely to witness anything which it would embarrass her to have him see and hear. Moreover, Smith, as revealed in her human and feminine aspects, interested him enormously. As a final consideration for keeping him in his place, he realised that should he attempt to withdraw before they passed into the pantry on their way to the back entrance, he would run a serious chance of being discovered, which would be unhappy all around. So he held his ground.

Smith surveyed Fletcher after his extremely personal question had been shot at her and replied calmly, "I haven't got anything against you."

"I'm steady," the young man continued.

"But steadiness isn't everything in a man," the girl replied.

"Now that's just like a woman," Fletcher exclaimed indignantly. "If you're steady, they want you wild; if you're wild, they want you steady!"

Freeman smiled inwardly and as a man sympathised with Fletcher in his resentment of the wrong which woman is continually doing his sex. He wondered how Smith would meet it. She looked up for a moment, tossed a mended sock into her basket and took a fresh one from the pile. "I'm sorry for that donkey," she said gravely.

Fletcher looked at her in open-mouthed surprise, a surprise that Freeman shared with him. "What donkey?" he demanded.

There was a gleam in Smith's eyes, but not even the corners of her mouth twitched. "The donkey whose hind leg you could talk off," she answered.

Fletcher made a gesture of impatience. "Now, look 'ere," he said, "for the third time of asking. I've got twenty-five bob a week and there's the window cleanin' and the Christmas boxes and the tips."

"I tell you I'm thinking of it," said Smith. "I can't do more than that."

"Wot's service?" Fletcher continued contemptuously,—"work, work, work, and no thanks for it!"

"But," she answered seriously, "it wouldn't be all play, play, play, if I was married."

"Well, you'd be working for yourself," Fletcher retorted. There was silence for a moment, then he went on: "We could make a nice little 'ome downstairs."

"I don't know that I want to live all my life in a basement," Smith observed with a return of feminine perversity in her manner.

"Well, where do you want to live?" demanded Fletcher.

"That," she said soberly, "is my business."

Fletcher looked at her in dismay. "Do you mean you won't?" he asked bitterly.

"Bless the man!" exclaimed Smith petulantly; "I don't mean anything. I don't say *yes* and I don't say *no*. If you don't like to leave it at that, you can take yourself off, you and your steps and your dirty water."

"All right! all right!" said Fletcher conciliatingly; "I won't hurry you." A thought came to him and he went on: "You wouldn't come to a music hall with me my next evenin' off, would you?"

Smith smiled. "Perhaps I couldn't get out," she said.

"Well, if you could?" said Fletcher.

"Well, I might if you pressed me," Smith replied. "But mind, it wouldn't mean 'yes.'"

"It wouldn't mean no, either, would it?" he rejoined.

"It would mean that I was making up my mind," said Smith with decision. She began to gather her mending together as if to indicate that the interview was ended and Fletcher started with his ladder and pail for the pantry door; but half way he stopped and turned back.

"You don't dislike me, do you?" he asked.

Smith looked up in wrathful surprise at seeing him again. "You take those things away and go and have your dinner," she said.

Fletcher faltered. "There's no getting a straight answer out o' you to anythin'," he said complainingly.

"I don't dislike you more than I dislike anybody else," said Smith bluntly.

Fletcher half smiled. "Well, that's better than a poke in the eye with a blunt stick," he said, "ain't it?"

"I suppose it is," said Smith.

"Good mornin' to you," said Fletcher.

"Good morning," said Smith.

She had risen and was holding the pantry door open for him while he edged through with his unwieldy step-ladder and pail. Freeman saw that she intended to go back to her mending, so he took advantage of the opportunity and slipped back through the passage to the drawing-room, amused at what he had witnessed and oddly enough as much interested as amused. He had never seen Smith, the woman, before, only Smith, the parlour maid. And the woman impressed him as much as the parlour maid. Moreover, the scene further interested him because Fletcher was engaged in the same quest as himself, the search for a wife. Mentally, he wished him good luck, for he had a fellow feeling for the energetic porter; but he didn't wish him luck in getting Smith. He had a curious feeling that Smith was too good for a dozen Fletchers.

FREEMAN ESSAYS CONVERSATION

CHAPTER VI

FREEMAN ESSAYS CONVERSATION

As Freeman pondered over the comedy that he had just witnessed, an impulse came to him to go back and see if he could surprise the central figure in it before the human Smith could wholly withdraw into the official. The approaching lunch hour gave him a reasonable excuse for appearing in the dining-room unsummoned. So he threw away his cigarette and went as quietly as possible down the passage. It was only as he parted the curtains that she heard him. She rose at once and began to gather her work into the mending basket.

To his amusement, he felt curiously embarrassed and obviously much less at ease than Smith. "Don't move," he said.

"I brought my work in here, sir," she began, "because the light is better. In these flats you can't see to do anything at the back."

He glanced at her and took in the situation with disappointment. The commanding, masterful, feminine Smith had vanished. There was only the precise and finished parlour maid, who made him feel ill at ease in spite of himself and without knowing why. His impulse was to flee, but pride and curiosity held him. He determined to conquer the awkwardness of the situation. After a pause, he succeeded in framing a sentence. "Those look suspiciously like some things of *mine*," he said, and picked a pyjama jacket off the pile.

"Yes, sir," said Smith.

"Did my—did Mrs. Dallas-Baker tell you to mend them?" he asked.

"No, sir," she answered. He had a suspicion that the human Smith wore the shadow of a smile lurking behind the mask of the parlour maid, but he had no way of proving it. "They were in such a state, sir," she continued, alluding to the pyjamas, "that

I thought I had better try and do something with them."

The answer was so complete that again Freeman was at a loss. The conversation seemed to be as completely ended for him as it had been for the wretched Fletcher. But he made a fresh, desperate start. "Do you often do work that you're not told to?" he asked.

"When I see a thing that wants doing," Smith replied, "I try to do it."

"That's not the way to get on in service," he ventured.

She glanced at him from the corner of her eye to reassure herself, then without looking up answered, "I don't like to see a gentleman go about in rags."

Freeman inspected the garment before him and smiled. "I am afraid that some of my things *are* in rather a beastly state," he observed.

"Well, the truth is, sir," said Smith candidly, "it's just a waste of labour mending them." She picked up a sock from the pile, ran her hand into it and showed it to him, a network of holes. "Look at that, sir," she exclaimed.

"I suppose I had better buy some more, hadn't I?" said Freeman somewhat abashed. "I hadn't realised how bad they were."

"Well, sir," said Smith, "I don't think it would do you any harm."

"I'll make a memorandum of it," Freeman said determinedly. "I'll get a half a dozen pairs of socks this very day."

Smith looked up from her work on the pyjamas and corrected him respectfully but firmly: "If you'd excuse my saying it," she said, "I'd get a dozen while you're about it, sir. It makes them last ever so much longer."

Freeman laughed softly. "All right," he assented, "I'll get a dozen pairs."

"And you want some pyjamas badly, sir," she added.

"Very well," he said, "I'll get some pyjamas. Anything else?"

"Nothing that I think of now, sir," she

replied, "except—" she added, glancing at the clock, "are you ready for your lunch, sir? Mrs. Dallas-Baker is lunching out with Mrs. Pemberton. She told me to tell you, sir."

"She told me she was lunching with Mrs. Parsons-Pratt," he remarked. "But that is immaterial. I'm quite ready for my lunch whenever the cook is."

"Very good, sir," she said. She gathered her sewing materials with one of her swift, efficient movements and disappeared into the pantry, and Freeman seated himself at the head of the table, where a single place had been set. His effort to discover Smith, the human and feminine being, had not been as futile as he might have expected, thanks to the accident of the socks and pyjamas, but now that he was being served at lunch, he foresaw that even such a mild bond of sympathy as garments in need of mending would be severed. And he was right. Smith returned shortly with shirred eggs, toast in a toast rack, then an entrée and a hot plate, all of which she placed accurately in their proper places and in professional silence. Twice he ventured a remark, harking back to the socks, but it secured merely the scantest "Yes, sir." Finally she asked him if he would drink hock or claret and he said, "Hock, please." While she was pouring it, he began to consider the curious tyranny which the relation of master and servant, as upper class life understands it, imposes upon both. There, for example, was Smith, standing beside him silent, attendant upon his wants. As long as he accepted her as a ministering piece of machinery and could ignore her presence, as one does the ticking of the clock or the crackling in the fireplace, they were both quite at their ease, he with his thoughts and she with hers. However, the moment that he began to regard her as a personality and to wish to be considerate of her as a woman, he would make them both uncomfortable. He foresaw what would probably happen, but nevertheless, in a spirit of inquiry, he resolved to go ahead and attempt to dismiss her from the room on grounds of consideration. "Smith," he said, "you needn't wait, if you don't want to. Everything is here, and I can ring when I'm ready."

"Thank you," said Smith, but she did not move.

"Do you like to stand there and watch me eat?" asked Freeman.

"I like to do things properly, sir," she replied.

"Just as you like," he said shortly.

"If you'd rather I didn't wait, sir," she began and then hesitated.

"I wish you to please yourself," said Freeman. "Do I make myself clear?" She made no answer, and after a pause he added, "Will you give the cook my compliments and tell her that these eggs are excellent?"

"Thank you, sir," said Smith.

There was another pause and Freeman felt that his experiment was failing. The ground that he had gained with the socks and pyjamas was slipping away from him. In desperation he went back to it. "I'm very much obliged to you for looking after my linen," he said. He knew that the effort was poor, but it was the best that he could think of.

Again Smith said, "Thank you, sir," and nothing else.

"I've not had anyone to do that sort of thing for me for a long time," he went on.

Smith received this information in silence and offered him a second helping of the entrée.

"No, thank you," he said. He swallowed a glass of hock and, looking up desperately, remarked, "Jolly weather, isn't it?"

"Yes, sir," said Smith.

Freeman felt that it was something to have won this concession from her, so he pressed his advantage immediately. "It's rather dull, eating alone, isn't it?" he observed.

"Some people mind it and some don't," she replied, and offered him a cutlet.

"I suppose that is so," he said. "I mind

"Smith received this information in silence."

it. You don't mind my making a few attempts at conversation, do you?"

"Not if you wish it, sir," said Smith politely.

"You see, you mustn't expect too much of me," he went on apologetically. "I've been away too long."

She had finished giving him his vegetables, refilled his wine-glass and had retreated to the end of the sideboard, where she stood sedately, so to speak, "at attention." There was a long silence and Freeman was conscious of utter defeat, when suddenly Smith of her own accord spoke. "Excuse me, sir," she said, and then broke off hesitatingly. Freeman stopped eating and looked up. "Excuse me, sir," she repeated, "is Rhodesia far?"

"It is rather," he said carelessly. His attitude was that of the man who is luring a shy child to him by an affectation of indifference.

"Farther than Australia?" Smith asked again.

"I don't know," said Freeman. "Why?"

"I was thinking," said Smith.

Freeman had an inspiration. "Your father is a farmer, isn't he?" he asked.

"Yes, sir," said Smith.

"And so am I, you know," said Freeman.

"I expect you farm a lot of land," she suggested.

"Two thousand acres," he answered.

He watched the effect that acreage made upon her. For the first time in his presence her professional self-consciousness slipped away and she spoke as the farmer's daughter. "That makes the difference," she said. "They say you can't make farming pay unless you do it on a big scale."

"Perhaps that is so," he answered. "Why did you go into service," he went on, "instead of helping your father?"

"Oh, we've all gone out, sir," she answered. "There are too many mouths to feed at home and father has enough to do to make both ends meet."

"Do you like being a parlour maid?" he asked.

"One has to do what one can, sir," she answered.

"Why don't you go to Rhodesia?" he suggested after a pause. "Able-bodied young women are worth their weight in gold there."

"I was thinking of it," said Smith quietly.

Freeman looked up in surprise. "Thinking of going to Rhodesia?" he asked.

"No, sir," she answered naïvely and obviously at a loss to account for his surprise. "I don't know anything about Rhodesia. I've got a sister married in Sydney and she says I can stay with her till I get something to do. She was a cook and one of those agencies got hold of her and took her out." She suddenly broke off, realising that he had finished his cutlet, and with a little motion of self-reproach offered him the dish again.

"No, thank you," he said. "What were you saying about your sister?"

She was still self-reproachful for her breach of professional duty. "I forget, sir," she said apologetically, "when I begin talking."

"Oh, that doesn't matter," said Freeman; "fire away!"

"I don't know what Mr. Thompson would say," she replied doubtfully, "if he caught me talking to a gentleman while I was waiting at table."

"Who's Mr. Thompson?" demanded Freeman.

"He was the butler in my first place, sir," she replied, "and he trained me."

"Well," said Freeman smiling, "I think there is every reason to believe that Mr. Thompson isn't in the least likely to find out. If that's a sweet you're bringing me," he added, "I won't have it at any price. Give me a little bit of cheese."

"Very good, sir," Smith assented and brought him the cheese.

"Now," said he, "go on about your sister."

"I don't think the mistress would like to

have me talk to you," she replied in a tone of doubt.

"Then I shan't eat any cheese," said Freeman.

For the first time she smiled a shy, faint smile and dropped her eyes. "Well," she said, "my sister hadn't been in Sydney three months before a gentleman asked her to marry him. He was a cab proprietor, and now she can ride in forty-three cabs, if she likes." She paused to fill his glass again. "I wrote and told her," she went on, "that she's carriage folk now and no mistake."

Freeman laughed. "And has she got a cab proprietor waiting for you?" he asked.

"They're not all cab proprietors in Sydney," she answered with a tinge of regret in her tone.

"No," said Freeman, "I suppose not. I expect that there would be some congestion of the traffic if they were."

"And they couldn't all make a living, could they, sir?" suggested Smith quite innocently.

Freeman nodded. "They would be reduced to driving one another about," he said.

After a pause, in which Smith seemed to be mentally contemplating the male population of Sydney driving one another about in cabs, she looked at Freeman again. "My sister says I'd marry in six months, if I liked," she said simply.

"Have you taken a ticket yet?" he asked.

"I'm in no hurry, sir," she answered.

"But you ought to marry," said Freeman. "That's what young women are made for."

Smith looked at him with the ghost of a smile again. "I don't need to go to the other side of the world to do that," she said.

"Hum," said Freeman. "That sounds as if you had something in view not very far from London."

"Well, sir, I may have, and I may not," she answered respectfully but with unmistakable firmness.

Freeman looked at her questioningly. "I suppose you wouldn't tell me who it is?" he said.

She made no reply, suddenly noting that he had stopped eating. "You've finished your cheese, sir?" she asked.

"I'll have an apple," he said. "You needn't bother about changing my plate." She offered him the apples and he took one. "Well?" he asked, "are you going to tell me?"

"Here I am talking again, sir," said Smith, self reproachfully.

"It helps my digestion," he answered. "Please continue."

"Well, sir," she began, "there *is* a young fellow who has asked me to have him, and of course if I do, I shan't go to Sydney."

"Do you like him?" asked Freeman.

"Yes, sir, I like him," said Smith, "but I don't know if I like him well enough to marry him. He always makes me laugh at the things he says."

"That's not a bad thing in a husband," Freeman observed.

Smith considered the idea for a moment. "But I don't know if I should laugh at them if I heard them all day long," she answered.

"Ah," said Freeman gravely, "that's always the danger of marrying a humourist."

Smith nodded. "And the worst is," she went on, "that he gets so cross when I say 'chestnuts.'"

"That's exactly it," said Freeman; "humourists are very touchy. They look upon it as a personal affront if you've heard their jokes before." He took his cigarette case from his pocket, opened it, and looked about for matches. In a moment she had put them beside him.

"If you're ready, I'll get your coffee, sir," she said, and disappeared into the pantry.

Freeman filled his lungs with the pleasant smoke and smiled. "Well," he thought to himself, "she can be almost human even with me." But what was uppermost in his mind was not the thought that he had achieved a triumph in making the professional and impersonal Smith a human being, but that she was a human being of such unusual dignity and sweetness and character. His meditations were presently broken in upon, however, as he heard someone opening the front door and entering the hallway. He pushed back his chair, and called, "Is that you, Rose?" Dallas-Baker's voice answered him.

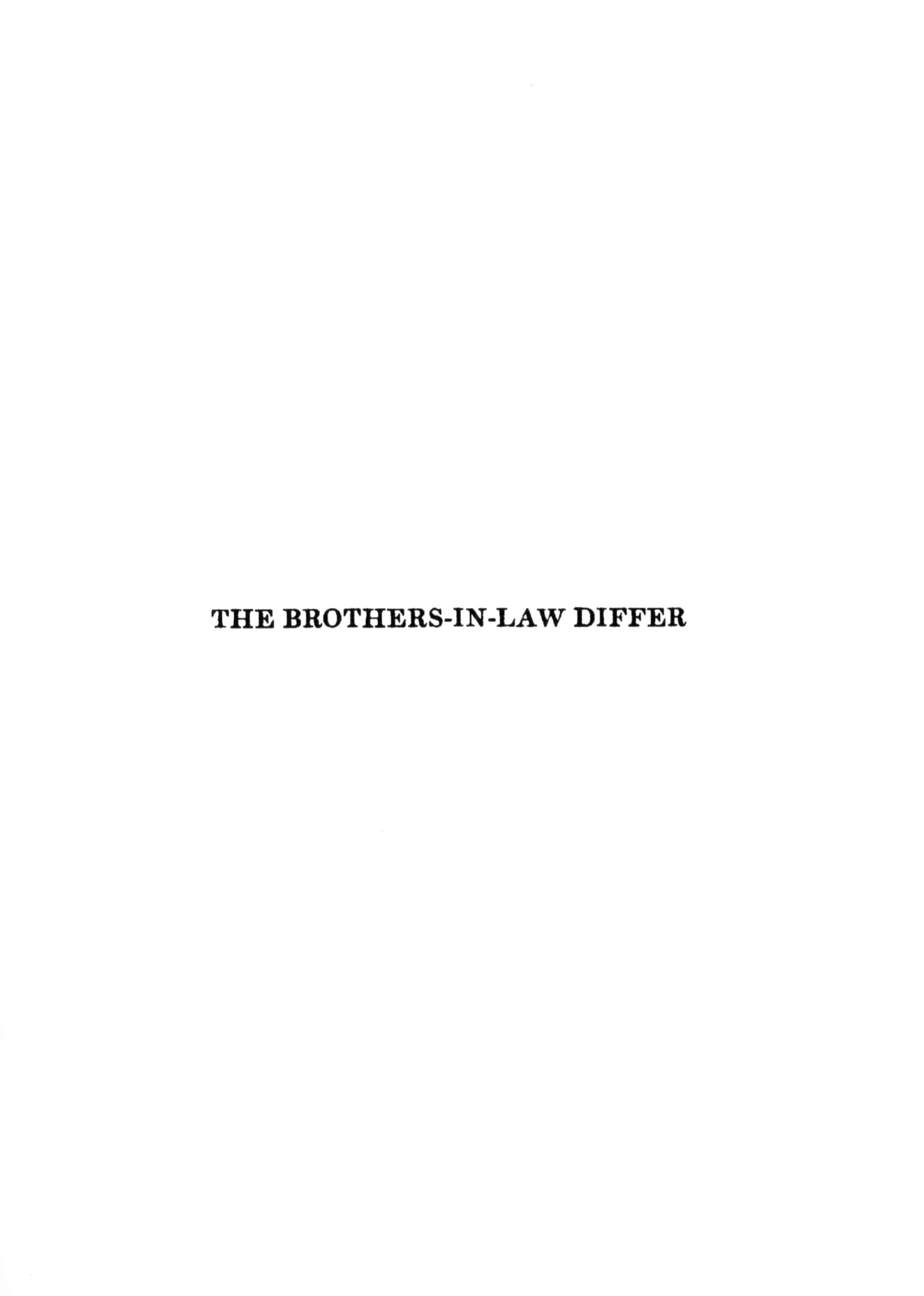

THE BROTHERS-IN-LAW DIFFER

CHAPTER VII

THE BROTHERS-IN-LAW DIFFER

"Hello," said Freeman as Dallas-Baker came into the dining-room, "are you back?"

"Yes," said his brother-in-law. "The case I was in came to a sudden end, and I thought I'd come home."

"You'll have some coffee?" suggested Freeman, for Smith had returned with the coffee things, again the silent, perfect parlour maid."

"No," said Dallas-Baker; "I've already had mine. I lunched in Hall. I didn't expect to find anyone in."

"You knew Rose was lunching out?" observed Freeman.

Dallas-Baker nodded and lit a cigarette.

"Who is this Mrs. Pemberton that she is lunching with? I don't think I've met her?" Freeman asked after a pause.

Dallas-Baker raised his eyebrows. "Mrs.

Pemberton?" he said. "Did she say she was lunching with Mrs. Pemberton?"

"Well, there may be some mistake," said Freeman. "She told me this morning that she was lunching with somebody named Parsons-Pratt, I think, but she left word with Smith that it was Mrs. Pemberton."

Dallas-Baker laughed softly. "Bless me," he said, "but how Rose does love her little mysteries. Why, I stopped into the Ritz not twenty minutes ago, and saw her lunching with Algy."

"With Algy?" said Freeman, and his face clouded.

"Certainly," said his brother-in-law. "Why not? They didn't happen to see me, but I saw them very distinctly at a table by the window."

Freeman was silent for a moment, waiting for Smith to leave the room with the dishes she was taking from the serving table. When she had gone he turned to his brother-in-law. "Herbert," he said, "how do you explain this? She gives the names of two different women whom she says she is engaged to lunch with and then goes to a restaurant with Peppercorn."

"I don't explain it," said Dallas-Baker calmly. "I accept it. It is possible, of course," he added, "that she had intended lunching with the women she named, or it is possible that she did not care to tell you she was lunching with Algy and got mixed in her excuses."

"But you appear to be strangely indifferent," Freeman answered.

"I'm the model husband," said Dallas-Baker; "I make a point of never interfering."

Freeman glanced over his shoulder to make sure they were alone and then drew his chair nearer to his brother-in-law. "Herbert," he began, "I have been wanting to have a talk with you for several days, but have hesitated from a natural unwillingness to be told to mind my own business. This circumstance, however, forces me to speak out."

"My dear fellow," said Dallas-Baker, "what is it?"

"Well," said Freeman, "do you think it's —let's call it *wise* to let Rose go about so much with this Peppercorn?"

Dallas-Baker looked at him in surprise. "Why shouldn't she?" he demanded.

Freeman hesitated. Dallas-Baker's surprise embarrassed him. "Well," he began, "I've been here a fortnight. Not a day has passed without that young man coming here to at least one meal. I never come into the flat without finding him sprawling about, and when he's not here it's because he's out with Rose."

"Rose likes him," said Dallas-Baker simply.

"That is a fact that could hardly escape anyone's observation," said Freeman coldly.

"But I like him, too," said Dallas-Baker. "He's just as much my friend as he is Rose's."

"Ah, I see," said Freeman; "that increases my difficulty in discussing the matter."

"And she does him good," Dallas-Baker went on. "It's the very best thing for a young man to go about with a woman older than himself."

"If I were in your place," said Freeman gravely, "I should think the toe of my boot would be a damned sight better for him than the uninterrupted society of my wife."

Dallas-Baker looked at Freeman in surprise. "But you don't suggest," he said, "that I should—" He stopped in annoyed amazement.

"Kick him out?" said Freeman, finishing the suggestion for him. "I do, indeed."

"But I've no reason to do anything of the kind," said Dallas-Baker with some warmth. "He's always been charming to me. Besides, Rose wouldn't hear of it."

"Rose can be brought to see that she's making a fool of herself," said Freeman.

"But I like him," said Dallas-Baker. "I'm very much attached to him."

"Well, I suppose there is no accounting for taste," said Freeman.

Dallas-Baker laid his half burned cigarette on the ash tray. "Tom," he began, "if you will forgive my saying so, I think this is a matter in which you are not capable of judging. You've been living in a primitive state where men are tyrants and women chattels. Your ideas are all very well in Rhodesia, but this is London."

Freeman rose and pushed back his chair. "My dear fellow," he said, "in London, Bulawayo or Kamchatka there is only one result of throwing a young man and a young woman in one another's society all day long."

Dallas-Baker also rose and pushed his chair back with a movement of impatience. "Nonsense," he said sharply. "We live in a highly civilised community. We've got ten thousand interests to occupy us. Algy has never thought of Rose in that way."

"Then all I can say," said Freeman, "the more fool he."

"What!" exclaimed Dallas-Baker astoundedly.

"I mean what I say," replied Freeman steadily. "Rose is a pretty woman. She is well dressed and very jolly. If the young man can be with her morning, noon and night with all the advantages of a complacent husband who sits by and twiddles his thumbs, and he doesn't make love to her, he must be a contemptible ass."

"But you are contradicting yourself," said Dallas-Baker warmly. "You're grossly contradicting yourself."

"No, I'm not," said Freeman. "With decent, normal people friendship between the sexes is impossible. It either leads on to love or it follows it."

"Either an *hors d'œuvre* or a savoury, I suppose," suggested Dallas-Baker ironically.

"If you like," said Freeman. "It's the fact, state it as you please."

"Tom," said Dallas-Baker in a tone of vexation which he had not shown before, "Rose knows quite well how to take care of herself. After all, I know her better than you do, I suppose. She is my wife as well as your sister."

Freeman nodded. "If she weren't," he said drily, "you can bet your boots I shouldn't be discussing her with you."

"But you don't understand," said Dallas-Baker more conciliatingly. "She's not at all the sort of woman to do anything silly. She takes no interest in love and that kind of nonsense."

"Surely," said Freeman savagely, "she has her five senses like other women."

"Of course she has her five senses," Dallas-Baker answered, "but they are spiritualised, they're—" he tried for the word he wanted and broke off in exasperation— "You're so coarse!" he cried.

"That may be," said Freeman calmly. "It is far better that they should be decent, normal people and break every commandment in the decalogue than the monsters you represent them. They must be beneath apes."

"Come! come!" cried Dallas-Baker hotly.

"This is going too far! This is beyond a joke. Beneath apes!" he repeated angrily. "I don't know what you mean. It's monstrous. Upon my soul, you've got no right to bring Rose into such a discussion!"

"It seems to me," said Freeman, "that when a woman says she has engagements to lunch with two different women and then lunches alone with a man that she makes herself a subject for discussion. You may be sure that if her husband and brother don't talk about her other people will."

"But don't you understand," said Dallas-Baker impatiently, "that those foolish little make believes are part of the game? They do no harm. She knows you don't like Algy, and very likely she said what she did merely to save you the annoyance of knowing that she was lunching with him."

"That is a very interesting explanation," said Freeman, "but if I were her husband, it would not satisfy me, and I am not satisfied with it as her brother." He stopped as he heard the front door. The next moment Rose and Algy came into the dining-room.

"Good heavens!" exclaimed Rose. "Your voices can be heard all over the building! What are you talking about in here of all places? It's nearly three o'clock."

"Nothing at all," said Dallas-Baker. "Nothing's the matter." He turned to Freeman and added sulkily, "A joke is a joke, but there are limits." Having delivered this parting shot, he swung round on his heel and went out.

Rose cast a look of half amused wonder about her and followed him.

Mr. Peppercorn glanced from one to the other of his disappearing hosts and then to Freeman. "I can't help thinking," he observed calmly, "that you've been trying to make yourself amiable."

"Right," said Freeman, "and apparently my efforts haven't met with the success they no doubt deserved."

"I expect your touch *is* a little elephantine," observed Mr. Peppercorn.

Freeman smiled good-humouredly. "You can't expect me to have such a facility for small talk as you who make a business of it."

"*Art,* not business, my dear fellow," corrected Mr. Peppercorn. He dropped languidly into the chair by the fireplace and sighed.

"I hope you find it a profitable one," said Freeman.

"It is my only means of livelihood," replied the youth, "and, as you see, I go to a tolerable tailor." He got up impudently, turned around to show the fit of his coat, and dropped into the chair again. "Also," he continued, "I am able to lunch at the Ritz when the fancy seizes me."

"But then," said Freeman blandly, "unless I'm mistaken, you allow your companion to pay the bill."

Mr. Peppercorn made neither denial nor affirmation. He busied himself in selecting a cigarette from his case.

"Haven't you been lunching at the Ritz

to-day with Rose?" Freeman went on with deliberation.

"I have," said Mr. Peppercorn.

"And didn't she pay the bill?" asked Freeman.

"She did," he replied.

Freeman looked at him contemptuously. "I'm afraid you'll think me unreasonably squeamish," he said, "but I shouldn't like to have a meal stood me by a woman. It would make me feel uncomfortably like one of the alien gentlemen for whom the police provide a ticket for the Continent and an escort to Charing Cross."

Mr. Peppercorn laughed, but not very mirthfully. "You're too absurd," he said. "Why on earth shouldn't Rose ask me to lunch with her at a restaurant as much as in her own house?"

"Can you tell me why she should ask you to lunch with her at all?" said Freeman.

"Certainly," said Mr. Peppercorn, who had quite recovered his usual composure.

"She finds me useful, entertaining and instructive."

"Really?" exclaimed Freeman, feeling more amazement than he cared to show. "I suppose you have been helping her try on a frock this morning."

"No," said Mr. Peppercorn. "Not frocks this morning. We bought half a dozen pairs of stockings and then went on to the National Gallery. Ever been there?"

"How old are you?" Freeman demanded after a pause.

"Twenty-eight," said Mr. Peppercorn promptly, "but I think I look less."

"You appear healthy enough and fairly strong," Freeman continued musingly. "Haven't you ever done any work?"

"I once was in a motor car business," Mr. Peppercorn replied, "but it went to smash."

"And do you consider doing anything else?" Freeman inquired with exaggerated civility.

"I'm vaguely looking out for another

motor car business," Mr. Peppercorn replied, "but have nothing immediately in view."

"That seems to be the refuge of every incompetent wastrel in the Kingdom," Freeman observed with some bitterness.

"In Europe, my dear fellow," corrected Mr. Peppercorn blandly.

Freeman looked at him and shook his head. "I should have more patience with you, Algy," he said, "if you were a fool pure and simple, but you're not that."

"Ah, now you flatter me," Mr. Peppercorn answered. "I must be on my guard."

"Yes," Freeman went on, "you're shrewd enough in your way. I daresay you could make quite a decent living if you tried."

"My dear fellow," said Mr. Peppercorn, flicking the ashes of his cigarette toward the fireplace, "we're taught to do our duty in that state of life in which a merciful providence has placed us. The civilisation of the present day has given rise to a variety of professions; and I have adopted one which is not nearly so well paid as it should be, considering how essential it is to modern society."

"And that is?" inquired Freeman attentively.

"It is too new to have a definite name," replied Mr. Peppercorn, "but those who follow it are known either as poodle dogs or tame cats."

"At least you have no false shame," said Freeman.

"Why should I?" replied Mr. Peppercorn. "I am a benefactor of my species. What do you suppose Rose and Herbert would do without me? I shop with Rose and take her to the play when Herbert has briefs to read. On Sundays I play golf with Herbert, and I play just well enough for him to beat me on the last green. If Rose is unwell, I play piquet with him in the evening. In return they make life pleasant for me. They take me away with them in the vacations, and when a tradesman duns me, neither Herbert nor Rose minds lending me a tenner."

"But are you under the impression that this sort of thing will go on forever?" said Freeman.

"Not at all," replied Mr. Peppercorn. "I find by experience that these jobs last about two years. I was two years with the Whitstables—of course the peerage adds to one's value afterwards, but it's not much catch. Lady Whitstable—" He paused, took the cigarette butt from the holder, blew through the latter and replaced it in its case. "Lady Whitstable," he went on, "wanted the earth, but she wanted it at a great reduction. After I left her I was two years with the Isaac Cohens. Give me the Cohens every time. Charming people!"

"Generous, I suppose," said Freeman.

"Quite," said Mr. Peppercorn, "and really not at all exacting."

"Well, and after two years?" said Freeman.

"They get sick of me," Mr. Peppercorn

replied. "I can't keep them on good terms with one another any more. And then they turn and rend me." He smiled broadly and went on. "I know all the signs a month or two beforehand, and I start looking out for somebody else."

"And you are content to go on in that way for the rest of your life?" demanded Freeman.

"I'm not thinking of it," replied Mr. Peppercorn frankly. "A tame cat like an actor should make his final bow before his public gets tired of him. One of these days, to-morrow or in ten years, I shall fall in love with a nice girl with about two thousand a year."

"But why should she marry you?" Freeman asked sceptically.

"Because I'm amusing," he replied, "or because I know nice people, or because I ask her. That is the commonest reason for which an heiress marries a pauper; and we shall live very comfortably on her money."

He stopped, and Freeman surveyed him with a curious, wondering contempt. "A parasite to the end," he said slowly, as if thinking aloud. "I'd rather sweep a crossing!"

Mr. Peppercorn regarded him with an amiable pity. "That's where we differ," he said. "I wouldn't."

"I'm afraid you will think me an awful donkey," Freeman observed, after a pause, "but I don't believe that you or anyone can get any permanent satisfaction out of life without working."

"My dear fellow," said Mr. Peppercorn, "that is too old-fashioned even for you. Believe me, regular employment is merely the hashish of the unintellectual."

Just then Smith came into the dining-room with a look of inquiry at the coffee cups that were still at the end of the table. "Clear them away," said Freeman. "We're going." He rose and led the way down the passage to the drawing-room, pondering on the contrast which two such characters as the efficient and wholesome-minded Smith and the effete and idle Peppercorn seemed to offer.

EMILY DISCLOSES HER INTENTIONS

CHAPTER VIII

EMILY DISCLOSES HER INTENTIONS

As Freeman and Algy came into the drawing-room they saw Dallas-Baker leaving it, and Rose standing by the fireplace, her face flushed and distorted with anger. The moment she saw her brother, she turned on him. "What have you been saying to Herbert?" she demanded.

Freeman made no reply, but glanced at Peppercorn.

"How dare you!" she went on. "It's infamous! How dare you interfere with me!"

Freeman turned to Algy. "Would you like to make yourself scarce, young man?" he said quietly.

Mr. Peppercorn smiled, settled himself in a comfortable chair, and began fumbling in his coat pockets for his cigarette case. "Not particularly," he replied. "I don't know of any spectacle more entertaining than a quarrel between nearest and dearest."

Freeman turned to his sister. "Will you tell him to go?" he asked.

"No," said Rose shortly.

"Well," said Freeman, addressing Mr. Peppercorn again, "it may surprise you, but I'm quite old-fashioned. I wash my dirty linen in private. You *must* clear out."

Without pausing in his search for a match, Mr. Peppercorn replied amiably, "I'm sorry, but I don't intend to."

Freeman bit his lip. "If you don't," he said in a very low voice that shook with anger, "I swear I'll knock you down and put you out."

"Then," said Mr. Peppercorn, looking him steadily in the eye, "I'm afraid you must knock me down. You are obviously much stronger than I, but this is an occasion when it is better to take a licking than knuckle under."

Freeman took a step backward and surveyed him in undisguised amazement. "Well, I'll be hanged!" he said.

Rose left the fireplace by which she had been standing and touched Peppercorn on the shoulder. "Please go, Algy," she said.

Mr. Peppercorn rose immediately and bowed low to her. "Certainly," he said in his most gallant manner. In the doorway he stopped and, looking back at Freeman, smiled triumphantly. "I never thought for a moment that you would hit me," he said. "A scuffle in a room with a woman in it— one talks about that sort of thing, but it doesn't come off." With that he bowed himself out and closed the door.

When he was gone, Rose turned to her brother. "Now," she said defiantly, "what have you to say to me?"

Freeman hesitated a moment. Then he held out his arms. "Look here, Rose," he said tenderly.

She backed away from him with a shudder of abhorrence. "For goodness' sake, don't touch me!" she exclaimed.

"Well," said Freeman, "sit down and let us talk quietly."

"Oh, I know what you are going to do!" she cried impatiently. "You are going to sentimentalise. You can keep all that to yourself."

He looked at her steadily and put his hands on her shoulders. "We shall understand one another better," he said, "if we make use of a little sympathy; don't you think so?"

With a twist of her body she threw off his hands and backed away from him again. "What has sympathy got to do with it?" she demanded. "We ask you to come and stay here. We tell you to treat the place like a hotel."

"If I had wanted a hotel," he put in, "I should have stayed at one."

"We make absolutely no claim upon you," she went on, ignoring his remark, "and now you can find nothing better to do than to fill my husband with absurd suspicions about Algy and me!" She broke off and, going to the window, threw it open, as if suffering for lack of air, and sat on the casement sill, breathing excitedly.

"Steady, Rose! steady!" Freeman said soothingly. "Don't forget that I spoke to you about it first and you refused to listen to me. I told you that I should go to Herbert."

"One says those things, but doesn't do them!" she cried impatiently and motioned away his attempt to take her hand.

"I'm awfully fond of you, Rose," Freeman began again. "What do you expect me to do when I see you behaving in a way that, that—" he stopped, embarrassed and at a loss to express what was in his mind.

"Well, what?" she demanded, "out with it."

"I'd rather not," he answered. "You are my sister."

She faced him for a moment in silence, and then began in a cold, measured voice:

"What right have you to preach to me? You set yourself up on a ridiculous pedestal—"

"Far from it," he interrupted, but she paid no heed to him.

"Don't you think that I know that father had to pay to get you out of a scrape with a woman at Cambridge?" she continued. "Don't you think I know what people said about you and Queenie Bishop?"

"If I came rather a cropper," he answered steadily, "that's no reason why you should come one, too."

"But what is it that you've got to reproach me with?" she demanded.

"Well," he said, "I think your behaviour with Algy Peppercorn is awfully indiscreet."

"Bah!" she exclaimed.

"But you must know that there can be only one explanation of it," he rejoined.

"What nonsense!" she said quietly. "You're so theatrical! Do you mean to say you think that there's anything really wrong between Algy and me?"

Freeman looked at her perplexedly. "My dear," he said, "how can you expect me to answer that question?"

"No," she insisted, "I ask it quite seriously; answer it."

"I hope with all my heart there isn't," he replied.

"That won't do," she said firmly. "Answer me yes or no."

"Well," he said, "if you insist, my answer is *yes*."

Rose burst into a scream of harsh laughter and sank back into the armchair near the fireplace. "Poor Algy!" she exclaimed. "I can't imagine anything that would bore him more than to make love to me."

He regarded her searchingly for a moment, wondering whether she was acting and then a sense of relief stole over him. At least he believed her. "Well," he said good-humouredly, "at all events I've made you laugh."

"Yes," she said. "You're really too ridiculous."

"Perhaps I am," he said thoughtfully, "but let us look calmly at the matter. If Algy doesn't make love to you, how much do you suppose he cares for you? He's only on the make, like the rest of your friends. If he came across a woman to-morrow, out of whom he could do a little better than out of you, he'd fling you aside like an old glove."

Her hesitation showed him that she shared in this view of Mr. Peppercorn. "Oh, well!" she answered, "I shall get tired of him long before he gets tired of me."

They were both silent for a time. Rose had leaned forward and was looking into the fire. He drew a chair next hers and sat down in it. "Will you let me say something to you," he began, "something that I have had on my heart almost ever since I came here?"

She made no answer and he put his hand out gently and took hers. "You know it's a rotten life you're leading, and these people you've got around you—what a poor lot they are! There's Cynthia—" he paused, trying to recall her name, and Rose prompted him.

"Rosenberg," she said.

"That's it," he went on. "Well, she's married a fat old German stockbroker for his money, and when her baby's ill she has the heart to leave it all day. She won't nurse it, because it would interfere with her amusements. Then there's Emily Chapman. She ought to have been married years ago."

"It's not for want of trying that she hasn't," Rose observed with a smile.

"I'm awfully sorry for her," said Freeman. "Her life consists merely of going from one bridge party to another. And do you think she gets any happiness out of it? You have only got to look into her eyes to see how restless and dissatisfied she is."

"She didn't treat you so well," put in Rose, "that you need waste any sympathy on *her*."

"I'm sure at heart she's a very decent girl," said Freeman. "If she could find a nice man—"

"Why don't you marry her yourself?" said Rose. "You are looking for a wife."

"What would she do on an African farm?" he answered hopelessly.

"I can't exactly see her as a farmer's wife," Rose assented.

"Still," said Freeman, "I'm not sure that she doesn't worry along as well as the rest of you. You are restless and dissatisfied, too, Rose, dear." He lowered his voice a little and went on very gently and seriously: "Don't you think you'd be far happier if you had children? It only means giving up a few selfish pleasures."

"I dare say I'll horrify you," said Rose bluntly, "but I prefer the selfish pleasures. The truth is, I don't want a child. It would bore me to death. I haven't the maternal instinct and there's an end of it."

He rose from his chair and stood with his back to the fire, looking down at her.

"Well," he said, "there can be nothing more to say then, can there?"

"Nothing," she answered. "I'm glad you appreciate it at last. We shall both be happier."

He looked at his watch and replaced it thoughtfully. "May I have the dining-room for a little while?" he asked. "I have some work to do and I should like to spread my papers on the large table."

"Of course," she answered. "Ask Smith to clear it."

He bent over her, kissed her on the forehead and went out.

When he was gone, she rose idly, went to the window, closed it again and took a cigarette from the silver box on the table. She was lighting it, when the door opened and Smith announced Miss Chapman.

"Well, my dear," said Emily, "how are you this delightful rainy afternoon?"

Rose finished lighting her cigarette, filled her lungs with the smoke and then replied, "I'm getting rather tired of Tom. I don't think I can stand his disapproval of everything I do much longer."

"Have you been having a row?" asked Emily.

"He's been lecturing me about Algy," Rose answered. "It's rather funny, isn't it, from Tom?"

Emily walked restlessly to the window and gazed out. "He's changed a good deal in the last eight years," she said.

"He's become quite impossible," said Rose. "I wish to goodness he'd find a wife and take himself off."

She smoked in silence, while the little clock on the mantelshelf ticked busily and Emily Chapman gazed out the window into the rain,—seeing nothing. At last Emily turned and came toward her. "Rose," she said, "would you hate me, if I married him?"

"Hate you, my dear?" cried Rose lightly. "You'd do me the greatest possible service."

"I suppose," said Emily, after a pause, "that you've told him that I've been twice engaged since he went away?"

Rose smiled. "No, of course not," she answered. "Why should I?"

"It would only have been natural," Emily replied. "But it was good of you not to. I know that you can queer the whole thing, if you like," she went on. "That's why I thought it would be better to speak to you first. I dare say you saw that I was thinking of it."

"I doubted if you had come here every day for a week merely to see me," said Rose.

Emily leaned down, put her hands on Rose's shoulders, and looked into her face. There was an anxious, appealing look in her eyes. "You wouldn't do anything shabby to me, Rose?" she said.

Rose smiled. "Of course not," she answered.

"Because," Emily went on, "if you've got anything against it, I won't even try."

"I haven't, honour bright," Rose replied. "What are you going to do?"

Emily shrugged her shoulders. "He's such a sentimentalist!" she said. "When a man is feeling so awfully sorry for you and wants you to get married—" she stopped and smiled.

Rose burst into a peal of laughter. "Upon my word, you *are* clever!" she exclaimed. "Why don't you beard him at his work in the dining-room this very afternoon?"

"I am thinking of it," said Emily calmly. "I have some business questions that I want him to answer, if you don't mind?" she added.

"You shan't be disturbed," said Rose amiably. She got up from her chair and smoothed back a lock of hair.

The two women faced one another for a moment. "Good luck," said Rose, and Emily went out into the passage and turned to the right toward the dining-room.

THE TRAP IS SPRUNG

CHAPTER IX

THE TRAP IS SPRUNG

Emily Chapman pushed open the dining-room door noiselessly and looked in. Smith was removing the cloth and Freeman, with a bundle of what appeared to be advertising pamphlets, was seating himself at the end of the table. He looked up, as he heard her, and smiled.

"Good gracious, how business-like you look!" she exclaimed. "I'll fly!" She made the pretence of retreating, and he rose and drew up a chair for her.

"Please don't go," he said. "They're only catalogues that I've got to look through. I wanted a place to spread them out, so that I could compare things. Thank you, Smith," he said. "This is capital."

"Do you wish anything more, sir?" asked Smith.

"No, thank you," he answered, and Smith disappeared.

"What are these things about?" asked Emily, referring to the catalogues. "Agricultural implements?"

Freeman's eyes had followed Smith as she went out through the pantry door, and she was still in his mind. "A nice girl, that," he said to Emily. "She's been talking to me."

"Rather forward, I should say," observed Emily.

"I asked her to," he answered. "It appears she wants to emigrate."

"Really?" said Miss Chapman.

"And very wise, too," observed Freeman. "In New South Wales she can get double the wages she can here, and she'll marry as soon as ever she wants to."

Emily's interest in Smith and her affairs seemed to increase. "You think that's the natural course for women, don't you?" she said seriously.

"I think they're happier when they carry out the purposes of nature," Freeman answered.

Emily looked away and began turning over the pages of one of the catalogues. "I suppose you have been buying all sorts of things," she said wearily.

"Not yet," he answered. "I ought to have been at it and haven't. Now I must hurry. My time is getting short."

"Why are you going so soon?" she asked, after a pause.

"Well, I don't want to leave the farm to its own devices longer than I can help," he answered. "Besides, it's my life. I want to get back to it."

"Are you happy out there?" she asked, after a pause.

"I never ask myself," Freeman replied. "I dare say," he added thoughtfully, "that is happiness."

Emily dropped into the chair that he had brought for her and was silent for a moment. Then, with a little break in her voice and with an evident effort, she spoke: "Lucky man!" she said.

Freeman looked at her pityingly and she

dropped her eyes. "You're not very happy, I'm afraid," he ventured.

She threw the catalogue that she was holding on to the table with a despairing gesture. "Wretched!" she murmured.

"I'm awfully sorry," said Freeman tenderly.

Emily smiled woefully. "It's very nice of you," she said. "But don't let's talk about it. It can do no good and it only makes things worse to talk about them."

"Come, now," said Freeman hopefully, "there is generally a way out of every difficulty."

She stretched out her hand, placed it lightly on his, and looked up gratefully at him. "I know you'd do all you could," she said, smiling with misty eyes, "but there's nothing you *can* do. There's nothing anyone can do."

"Won't you tell me what it is that is troubling you?" he asked.

"Oh, my dear friend," Emily replied, "it's nothing except that the years are passing one by one and that I'm wasting my life. I'm useless in the world, a burden to myself and to everyone connected with me."

"Oh, what nonsense!" he exclaimed impatiently.

"And I have brought it all on myself," she went on, "every bit of it. I have only myself to thank; but that doesn't make it any the easier to bear, does it?"

"Oh, come," he said, and smiled encouragingly. "There will be a way out."

She shook her head, rose, and began to walk slowly to and fro before the fire. "What sort of an opinion of myself do you think I can have?" she began in a low voice. "I was willing enough to marry you when you had money. I threw you over when you lost it."

"Are you thinking of that?" he asked in some surprise.

She nodded. "Can I ever forget it?" she said.

"We were a pair of young fools in those days," he said reassuringly.

"Still, I was old enough to know what I was doing," she replied. "You must despise me from the bottom of your heart."

"I do nothing of the sort," he answered stoutly. "Put that idea out of your head at once."

"You are very good and generous," she said. "Much too good."

"Nonsense!" he muttered, and there followed a silence, which Emily broke.

"Were you very much in love with me, then?" she asked.

He dropped his eyes. "Yes," he answered in a husky voice.

"How cruel and heartless I was!" she exclaimed brokenly. "But how I've paid for it! Oh, if you only knew how unhappy I am!" She turned her face away and began to sob.

Freeman rose and stood uncertainly. He was very much moved. "Oh, my dear," he said, "don't cry! I can't bear it." He went to her, took her hand, and held it, while her sobbing increased. "Please don't," he said.

She drew her hand away and endeavoured to get control of her voice. "Please go away!" she begged. "I'm only making a fool of myself. But, oh, I've been so bitterly punished!" She sank into the armchair by the fire and hid her face in her hands and began sobbing anew.

"For God's sake, don't cry!" he exclaimed. He seized her by the shoulders, half in command, half imploring, and he felt her tremble under his touch.

Presently she raised her face again and began in a choked, uncertain voice: "It was only after you went that—" she hesitated, but went on, "that I knew how much I loved you, and when I saw you again the other day—" She paused, as she saw Freeman wince. "Yes," she said meekly, "and it was nothing to you. I saw that you thought me old and plain and horrible. But you were just the same, and it all came back to me. If you wanted revenge, you've got it." She hid her face in her hands and sobbed convulsively.

"God knows," he said, in a voice that was hardly audible, "I never thought of any of those things. I was sincerely glad to see you, as I believed you were to see me, as old friends."

"Do you mean it?" she said. "Do you mean that you weren't glad that I had lost my looks, that things had gone wrong with me?"

"But what do you think me?" he exclaimed. "A monster?"

"You would only be human," she said, "if you enjoyed it, after the way I had treated you. But if you only knew the truth!" she went on. "Even at the time it brought as much suffering for me, as it did for you, and more; for I was in the wrong. Oh, if you only knew the misery of those years! I was expecting you to write. Every time the postman came, my heart was in my throat. I thought that men never took women at their word, that they always expected them to reconsider. I thought that you would, but you never gave me another chance."

Freeman, who had been listening in pained attention, looked into the fire. "I thought that you had forgotten all about me," he said simply.

"But I couldn't write," she said, "after the way I had acted. All I could do was to wait. I made up my mind to wait."

"You don't mean to say," he exclaimed, "that you've cared for me all this time?"

She looked at him steadily. "If I haven't married, it's on your account, Tom," she answered gravely. "I couldn't, that's all. I've never cared for anyone but you. I never shall."

He turned away to the window and gazed aimlessly out into the drizzle that was falling through the grey air, and she followed him with furtive, anxious eyes. As she saw him turn towards her again, she bent her head and hid her face in her hands.

"Emily," he demanded, "do you still care for me?"

"Oh, don't!" she answered brokenly. "How can you humiliate me?"

"There is very little love in the world," he said slowly. "A man ought to be very grateful, if a woman cares for him. Perhaps fate had just that in mind when it brought me back to England." He paused and waited, but she did not look up. "Do you understand what you are bringing on yourself?" he went on. "I'm a farmer in a new, untamed, unsettled country, and my life there is a hard, lonely one, and must be so for as many years as we can look ahead. It is very different from anything that you have known."

She raised her head and looked at him despairingly. "If you knew how lonely I am here!" she said. "There is not a soul in the world that cares for me!"

"Well," said Freeman, after a pause, "I have very little to offer you. If you will marry me, I will try to make you a good husband."

She said nothing for a time, and he remained before her, gazing down at her face. Presently she murmured his name in a broken voice and held out her hands to him. He was lifting her gently to her feet, when she heard the door knob rattle and drew away. A moment later Smith entered with a visiting card on a salver.

"A gentleman to see you, sir," she said to Freeman.

Freeman looked at the card. "It's the agent for one of these firms of agricultural implements," he said. "Tell him I'll see him directly."

"Very good, sir," said Smith, and went out.

"Well," said Freeman, when they were alone, "let's tell Rose and have a celebration."

"Please not now," she answered pleadingly. "Don't think it odd of me, but I must have a little time. Everything is so changed. I'm so happy. Perhaps Rose wouldn't altogether sympathise with me, you understand?"

"I think I do," he said gently. "You'll tell me when?"

"Let's wait a week," she said hurriedly. "I must be going, or Rose will suspect something." She turned and held both hands out to him. "You are the most generous man in the world," she said in a husky voice.

He took her hands, expecting to take her in his arms, but something changed his purpose—one of those subtle, inexplicable currents of feeling that rule our lives at moments of crisis. He bent low and raised her fingers to his lips, and then released her.

She seemed not to resent his action, and a moment later was gone.

The purpose of his visit was accomplished. The woman that he had once wanted above all the things of earth was his, yet a curious sense of disappointment weighed on him. "It is all for the best," he said to himself.

"It must be. It will come back to me. At five and thirty," he argued with himself, "a man doesn't respond to sentiment as at five and twenty." Anyway, sentiment was not what he was looking for. He needed a wife, and he had found one. He ought to be a very happy man.

Smith came into the room again, ushering in the agricultural implements man and passed close to him, as she crossed the room to the pantry door. And as she passed, something too thin and ineffable to be called a fragrance seemed to come from her clean, transparent skin, or from her mass of straw-coloured hair, or from some inner loveliness. Whatever it was, it sent a curious thrill through Freeman, and he turned to his business.

HOW A RUBBER AT BRIDGE WAS INTERRUPTED

CHAPTER X

HOW A RUBBER AT BRIDGE WAS INTERRUPTED

WHEN Emily left the dining-room, she had gone softly down the passage and had let herself out without speaking to Rose. As a not unnatural consequence, Rose concluded that something had "happened," but exactly what, she could not satisfactorily determine from Tom's actions. Rose really cared very little whether Emily married Tom or not. She had been honest in saying that she bore Emily no resentment and would keep her hands off, but she had a keen human curiosity to know what the outcome of the attack had been. For three days Emily kept away from Credinton Court. On the fourth, Rose called her on the telephone and insisted that she come to lunch and for bridge afterwards. Rose knew that Tom had promised to come in during the afternoon and she suspected that her best chance of finding out what apparently neither he nor Emily wished to talk about lay in watching them when they were together. Algy and Dallas-Baker were both in for lunch, so that Rose had no chance to speak to Emily alone. After lunch, they fell to immediately at bridge.

On the rubber game Emily laid down her cards when the hand was half played and showed that she had the rest of the tricks.

"You must be very unlucky in love, Emily," observed Rose pointedly. "I never saw anyone hold such cards!"

Emily met her look without flinching. "You ought to know," she said coolly.

"Well, luck always changes," Rose answered, "no matter what it is."

Mr. Peppercorn, who had been adding up the score, announced that the rubber was "thirty-five bob."

Dallas-Baker looked at his watch and rose. "I'm afraid that I must be going," he said. "Cynthia will be here directly to take my place."

"She ought to be here now," said Rose. Just then the telephone bell sounded shrilly in the passage outside. "Oh, that dreadful bell!" she exclaimed. "Go and see who it is, Herbert."

"Very well," said Dallas-Baker, and he went out.

"I hope it's not Cynthia," said Rose. "If she puts us off at this hour, I shall never forgive her."

Rose not only chafed at the idea of losing her afternoon's amusement, but she counted on Tom's presence during the card playing as a basis for her observations and inferences as to the results of Emily's campaign.

"But your husband *would* stay, if we needed him?" suggested Emily.

"No," said Rose, "he's got to go out. He's speaking at some silly political meeting."

"Then it's lucky that we were able to get hold of him to make our fourth until now," Emily observed.

"It is," said Rose. "Still, he has been

coming home to lunch rather often of late."

"It looks to me," said Mr. Peppercorn, "as if work was devilish slack at Lincoln's Inn. We shall have to start economising, Rose."

"It's dreadful, isn't it?" said Rose lightly. "And I want a car so badly."

"We truly ought to have one," said Algy. "I have heard of a jolly second-hand one that would just suit us. It's only been used three months."

"How much do they want for it?" Rose asked, but before Mr. Peppercorn had time to answer, Dallas-Baker came back. She looked up at her husband irritably. "Who was it?" she asked.

"Otto Rosenberg," he answered.

"How tiresome!" Rose exclaimed. "Isn't Cynthia coming?"

"I don't know," he replied. "Rosenberg wanted to know if Cynthia was here."

"I suppose," observed Mr. Peppercorn, "that she's out on the tiles and the old man is getting anxious."

Emily laughed. "What else could he expect when he married her?" she said.

"He is getting to be an unendurable bore," said Rose. "He rang up about one o'clock and asked if she was lunching here, and I told him no. Then he had the impertinence to ask me if I knew where she was lunching. It so happened that I did, but I told him I hadn't the least idea."

"You shouldn't have said that, my dear," said Dallas-Baker.

"And why not?" Rose retorted. "Has he any business trying to make me spy on his wife?"

"What do you suppose he is fussing about now?" Emily asked, after a pause.

"Oh, it's only that blessed baby," Rose answered. "It's always ill."

"Well," said Dallas-Baker, "have your own way, but I promised Rosenberg that we'd tell Cynthia the moment she came."

"That was rather silly," said Rose. "She can't do any good by going home, and a message like that will only worry her.

Otto's an old woman and he flies back from the city every time the child starts squalling."

"Still I think we ought to tell her, Rose," insisted Dallas-Baker. "Otto's very anxious that she should go home at once."

"We'll tell her after we've had a rubber," said Rose decidedly. "I don't see why our afternoon should be wasted because a peculiarly uninteresting baby isn't quite well."

"Hear! hear!" said Mr. Peppercorn.

"Well," said Dallas-Baker doubtfully, "I dare say that will do. It can't make much difference if she gets back an hour sooner or later. But I don't like the idea of deceiving him." He turned to go, when the door opened and Freeman came in, and Rose at once fixed her eyes on Emily Chapman.

"Hello, everybody," he called jovially. "At it again." He crossed the room to the card table and shook hands with Miss Chapman.

"Not at the moment," Emily answered lightly. "We're waiting for Cynthia Rosen-

A RUBBER AT BRIDGE 167

berg." Her manner was natural and without restraint or embarrassment. Rose could make nothing of it.

"You see," said Dallas-Baker, by way of explanation, "I've got to go before we could finish another rubber."

"His country calls," said Mr. Peppercorn, "and he is going to tell the British elector how to do his duty. Don't look at me," he added, "as if you had never laid eyes on me before. It's rude."

"I was wondering," said Freeman, "if I had seen you before to-day. Did you have breakfast here, to-day? I forget."

"No," drawled Mr. Peppercorn. "I always breakfast in bed. Mother thinks it's so much better for me. I came to luncheon."

"Then I've not seen you," said Freeman. "In that case, I wish you good morning."

"It's *too* kind of you," said Mr. Peppercorn.

"And may I express the hope," continued Freeman, "that you passed a good night?"

"I thank you again," said Mr. Peppercorn; "I slept the sleep of the pure at heart."

"The news," said Freeman with mock gravity, "fills me with satisfaction."

Mr. Peppercorn rose and bowed with ceremony. "If it were possible," he said, "to embarrass me, your politeness would cover me with confusion."

At this point the door opened and Smith announced Mrs. Rosenberg.

Exclamations of joy received her and she burst into the room and began to shake hands. "I'm fearfully sorry to be so late," she explained, "but I've had all sorts of things to do, and I thought I should never get away from lunch."

"We were beginning to be very cross with you," said Rose.

"You'll forgive me," said Mrs. Rosenberg, "when you know what I've been through."

"Tell us your woes!" said Mr. Peppercorn sympathetically.

"Well," said Mrs. Rosenberg, "I spent the entire morning at the dressmakers. Literally, I never got away until half-past one o'clock, and then I had to rush to the Ritz and lunch with Montie Kenyon. He, poor dear, is very much exercised over his last love affair and I had to listen to that until I thought I should die; then I made him go along to look at a private view with me which I had promised to turn up at, and then I had to make half a dozen calls, and here I am. I've never had such a rush in my life!"

"Rather an arduous day," observed Mr. Peppercorn, lighting a cigarette.

"Do you think a rubber will rest you?" asked Dallas-Baker uneasily.

"I know it will," Mrs. Rosenberg answered quickly. "The only thing that kept me going all day was the thought of a quiet rubber or two here before dinner."

"Parliament should take it up," said Freeman, who had been standing in the background. "There should really be an eight hour day for the idle rich."

Mrs. Rosenberg turned and smiled at him. "I didn't see you when I came in," she said. "Do tell me how you are getting on."

"Getting on? I?" he said perplexedly.

She smiled at him and began taking off her gloves. "Yes," she said. "Rose told me you'd come to England to look for a wife. I was thinking it would be such a chance for me to get rid of some of my sisters-in-law."

Rose shot a searching look at her brother and then at Emily, but neither of their faces gave her the information for which she was seeking.

Freeman smiled back at Mrs. Rosenberg. "Are they very attractive?" he asked.

"Very," said Mrs. Rosenberg, "and there are three of them. As long as you are going to South Africa or some such outlandish place, it occurred to me that you might marry them all."

"I'm afraid I'm a little late for such liberty of conscience as that," he answered. "Africa is no longer as liberal as it used to be. But, tell me more about these ladies."

"One," said Mrs. Rosenberg, "is called

Rachel, another Lydia, and the third Pom-Pom."

"I think I should like Pom-Pom," said Freeman. "Pom-Pom Freeman sounds very well, don't you think so? Go on about them," he added. "What do they do?"

"Well, principally," said Mrs. Rosenberg, "they spend their time in picking holes in me and pointing them out to Otto. They've got the strongest sense of other people's duty that I have ever come across."

Mr. Peppercorn smiled approvingly, but said nothing.

"That sounds rather like a warning," said Freeman. "A sense of duty, like charity, should begin at home."

"What have they been doing now?" Emily asked.

"Nothing new," said Mrs. Rosenberg. "The same old nag, nag. Their idea of a jolly life is that I should spend the whole day by baby's cradle, except for an hour in the morning, when I must run out and do the housekeeping. But," she went on, "I tell Otto, what on earth have we got seven servants for." She broke off suddenly and, turning to Rose, added, "You should see our new second footman, Rose, dear. He's six foot four. I'm so proud of him!"

"My dear," said Rose shortly, "I wish you would realise that one doesn't talk of one's second footman unless one is in love with him."

"Even then it is slightly indiscreet," suggested Dallas-Baker, with an elephantine effect at lightness.

"I'm not interested in the giant footman," said Mr. Peppercorn, "but I wish that you would tell me more about your sisters-in-law."

"Well," said Mrs. Rosenberg, "of course, they're Jewesses, but they aren't so bad, really, when you get to know them, and they've got thirty thousand pounds apiece."

Mr. Peppercorn's face lighted up.

Emily smiled and looked at Freeman. "That sounds rather a chance, Tom!" she said.

A RUBBER AT BRIDGE 173

"Doesn't it?" he replied, and again Rose glanced from one to the other of them and again she was unable to satisfy herself as to what had passed between them.

"I know that I shouldn't care for Pom-Pom," said Mr. Peppercorn. "It sounds rather affected. Did you say that they all had thirty thousand?"

Mrs. Rosenberg nodded.

"Then," continued Mr. Peppercorn, "if you will not think me bold, I shall put Lydia's name upon my cuff, so that I may memorise it at my leisure. I think it well to file Lydia for reference. Who can tell?" He produced a gold pencil and pretended to make the memorandum on his wristband.

Rose ran her hand over one of the packs of cards that lay on the table. "Cut for partners," she said. "If we want to play bridge, we really ought not to waste any more time."

Mrs. Rosenberg drew a card and then, glancing about, saw that there were five possible players. "But aren't you going to play?" she asked of Dallas-Baker.

"No," he answered. "I have to go." He took out his watch. "I must be off in ten minutes. That's why they were waiting for you. I shall just stop on to see you get started."

"I, for one, Herbert," said Rose petulantly, "shall be thankful when you go. It does bore me to see you take your watch out every other minute."

"It's quite true, Herbert," said Mr. Peppercorn amiably. "You've become distressingly restless of late, and we only married you because we liked your stolidity. Do look up the law and see if one can have a marriage annulled on the ground of false pretences."

Dallas-Baker laughed heartily. "Upon my soul!" he said, "I don't know what things are coming to." He glanced at Freeman, but Tom had gone to the writing table and was seating himself to write a note.

Mr. Peppercorn drew his card and displayed it.

"You and I, Algy," said Emily, "and we have the choice of seats."

"Take the ones with the armchairs," he replied unblushingly, "and let's have the red cards."

He had hardly begun to deal before the telephone began to ring again in the hallway and Rose sat up angrily, as if its ringing were a personal affront. "It's too exasperating!" she exclaimed. "There's that wretched telephone again!"

"Shan't I go?" asked her husband.

"Yes, do," she answered, "and afterwards you might take the receiver off. I don't want to be interrupted again."

"All right," he said and started for the door, when it opened and Smith entered.

She crossed the room noiselessly to Mrs. Rosenberg, and in her low, pleasant voice said: "You're wanted on the telephone, ma'am."

"Oh, how tiresome!" Mrs. Rosenberg exclaimed. "Have you said I'm here?"

"Yes, ma'am," said Smith.

"That's too stupid of you, Smith," cried Rose. "You should always say you'll inquire. I thought I had impressed that upon you before."

"Yes, ma'am," said Smith meekly.

"Well, say I'm in the middle of a hand at bridge," said Mrs. Rosenberg, "and that I can't possibly come. Ask them to give you the message."

"Very good, ma'am," Smith answered, and went back to the telephone.

Dallas-Baker looked nervously at his wife and caught her eye.

"You seem to be in great demand, Cynthia," Rose said chaffingly. "This is the third time that you've been rung up here."

"I suppose Otto has got some foolish idea in his head," Mrs. Rosenberg replied with a gesture of impatience. "I oughtn't to have told him that I was coming."

A RUBBER AT BRIDGE 177

"If one wants to play cards in peace and quiet," said Emily, "it's fatal to let anyone know one's whereabouts. They invariably ring you up when you are playing a very light no trumper and need all your wits about you."

Dallas-Baker, who had been standing by with a look of anxiety in his face, dropped into the chair next Mrs. Rosenberg and glanced over her hand. "As a matter of fact, Cynthia," he began, then he hesitated, as he felt Rose's look fixed upon him.

"Well?" said Mrs. Rosenberg, arranging her cards.

"The fact is," he began— Then he broke off, for Smith entered the room again.

Freeman had swung around from his seat at the writing table and watched her as she came in. He noticed that the colour had left her face and he ascribed it to the sharp rebuke that his sister had given her. "It's an outrage," he said to himself, "for one grown woman to speak to another in that way before people."

And for the moment a passion of resentment against Rose swept over him. But there was nothing that he could do, so he kept silent.

Smith came to Mrs. Rosenberg again. "If you please, ma'am," she began, and then stopped.

The four at the card table looked up in amazement. "What on earth is the matter with you, Smith?" said Rose, for Smith had stopped because she was unable to control her voice.

"I'll bet a fiver," said Mr. Peppercorn, "that Otto has eloped with the cook. The kitchen maid is giving notice."

"It's Mr. Rosenberg, ma'am," said Smith with an effort.

"Well?" said Mrs. Rosenberg impatiently.

"Oh, ma'am," cried Smith brokenly, "I can't tell you!"

"Smith," exclaimed Rose sharply, "you forget yourself!"

"You must go at once, ma'am," Smith went on. "It's—it's the baby."

"Oh, no, ma'am," said Smith, "please go at once."

Mrs. Rosenberg looked uncertainly at Rose. "I suppose Otto is in one of his states of mind again," she said. "I'll have to go. Tell Mr. Rosenberg," she said, turning to Smith, "that I'll come as soon as I have finished my hand."

"Oh, no, ma'am!" said Smith in a low, earnest voice that had a haunting, resonant tenderness, "please go at once. You mustn't go on; you really mustn't!"

Rose pushed her chair back indignantly and looked at her parlour maid, blazing with anger. "What on earth are you talking about?" she exclaimed.

Freeman had left the writing desk and joined the party at the card table. "Smith," he asked quietly, "what is it?"

"Oh, sir," she answered, "they said I was to break it to her."

"Yes," said Freeman gently, "I dare say that they thought it was my sister speaking. What is it?"

Her voice dropped almost to a whisper and the tears gathered in the corners of her violet eyes. "It's dead, sir," she answered.

Mrs. Rosenberg gave a curious little cry and the hand that held her cards dropped to the table. Then, without speaking, she rose and began mechanically searching for something. Peppercorn, divining that it was her gloves she wanted, found them for her under the table. As she passed Freeman on her way to the door, he made a motion as if to accompany her, but she waved him back with a nervous, frightened gesture, and went out.

Dallas-Baker broke the silence. "Oughtn't I to go with her?" he asked huskily of his wife.

Rose shook her head. She was white with fear. "No," she said, breathing hard. "Let Algy go."

Algy nodded. "I don't mind," he said, and followed Mrs. Rosenberg out.

Smith had remained speechless, with the tears brimming in her eyes. After Peppercorn had disappeared, Rose turned on her.

"What are you waiting for, Smith?" she asked sharply.

"Oh, ma'am," Smith answered brokenly, "isn't it dreadful!"

"For goodness' sake, go away!" cried Rose violently.

"I beg your pardon, ma'am," said the parlour maid, and crossed noiselessly and erect to the door, which she shut behind her.

Freeman had an impulse to follow her, but he checked himself. He saw Emily still sitting, dumb and expressionless, at the card table, with her cards clutched tightly in her hand.

EMILY SHOWS HERSELF IN A NEW LIGHT

CHAPTER XI

EMILY SHOWS HERSELF IN A NEW LIGHT

AFTER a few moments Rose dropped into her chair again, Dallas-Baker turned his back to the fire, and Emily laid her cards face downward on the table.

Freeman went back to his seat at the writing desk, took up his pen and sat with it idle between his fingers.

"I like Smith's idea of trying to break it gently," said Rose, trying to recover her usual voice and manner.

"She seemed quite upset," said Emily.

Dallas-Baker began nervously pacing the room. "I hope it won't lead to any unpleasantness," he said apprehensively.

Rose looked at him with an expression of impatience. "Oughtn't you to be going to your meeting?" she said.

He started and looked at his watch again. "I suppose I ought," he said apologetically.

"I had quite forgotten it for the moment." He looked about him uncertainly and then went out without speaking.

Freeman followed him with a perplexed look. When he had gone, he rose and came towards the two women, who were at the card table. "Rose," he said, "did you know the child was ill?"

Rose started. "They rang up just before lunch," she answered evasively, "to ask if I knew where Cynthia was."

"But you did," said Freeman. "I heard you say at breakfast that she was lunching at the Ritz."

"It's not my business to tell Otto where his wife is lunching," she replied sullenly.

"Still," said Freeman, "if you had, she might have been home three hours ago."

"But how could I," she answered, "when she had told me in confidence?"

"Was she lunching with anyone she shouldn't have been with?" asked Freeman.

"No," said Rose. "Otto doesn't like Montie Kenyon, but there's no reason why she shouldn't lunch with him, if she wants to."

"Then you ought to have told Rosenberg where she was," Freeman said slowly and authoritatively.

Rose sprang to her feet. "For goodness' sake, don't lecture me!" she exclaimed excitably. "I'm not in the mood to stand it."

Her brother looked at her thoughtfully for a moment, then an unpleasant possibility flashed upon him and a shadow crossed his face. "Rose," he said sternly, "you didn't refuse to tell Rosenberg where his wife was so that your bridge party shouldn't be broken up?"

"Good heavens!" answered Rose. "You don't suppose that I knew the child was dying, do you? Otto was always getting into a state of mind about its health. I hadn't any idea that it was really sick. The whole thing's a beastly nuisance."

Freeman gazed at his sister with something like horror as well as indignation in his eyes. "Why, Rose!" he exclaimed. "You don't mean—"

"For heaven's sake, let me alone!" she cried explosively. "You've done nothing but blame me for one thing or another ever since you came. I'm sick of it. If you're not satisfied with me, you can go!"

"Yes," said Freeman sadly, "that is the best thing I can do. I'm only a stranger to you. We speak a different language, you and I."

"And I can only hope," Rose answered, her anger rising hysterically, "that I don't speak such drivelling nonsense in mine as you do in yours. Oh, if you only knew how I loathed you," she went on. "How thankful I shall be when you go and how I hope I shall never, never see you again!" Her voice rose almost to a scream and as she finished she started for the door.

"You can easily be spared that!" he rejoined. "Of course, I'll go." He watched her as she flung herself out of the room and slammed the door behind her. "Well," he

EMILY IN A NEW LIGHT

said grimly to Emily, "you have witnessed a very pretty domestic quarrel."

"When a single woman has reached my age," Emily answered, "she's seen her fair share of them."

"Rose is the only relation I've got," Freeman went on after a pause, "and I came back fonder of her than I'd ever been before. I clothed her with all the qualities I want in a woman."

Emily smiled faintly. "Poor Rose," she said. "She was always a little overdressed before."

"Oh, no," he answered. "It was nothing very much that I expected. I asked only that she should be honest and truthful and a faithful wife and a good mother."

Emily watched him thoughtfully with a curious smile on her lips as he went on setting forth the essentials that he demanded of Rose. "I don't suppose that it is very much to ask," she observed, "and yet—" she hesitated and stopped, and looked at Freeman.

"But how could she be so wantonly cruel

and selfish?" he went on, disregarding the defence implied in Emily's hesitation. "The only person who seemed to care a damn was Smith."

"Persons of that class are very easily moved," Emily replied.

"It's easy enough to be unmoved, if you have no heart," he said fiercely.

Emily looked at him searchingly. "Let's be honest with ourselves," she said after a pause, "not sentimental. Do you really care twopence whether the child is alive or dead?"

He gave an exclamation of surprise and indignation. "Would it seem odd to you if I did?" he answered.

"After all," said Emily, "it's nothing to you. You have never even seen it."

"But the world is such a jolly place!" he exclaimed. "And life is so full and splendid! Think how hard it is that any child should be snatched away before he's enjoyed anything."

Emily began mechanically gathering the cards that lay spread upon the table. "Do you really think the world is a jolly place and that life is splendid?" she asked with a trace of irony in her tone.

"Don't you?" he answered.

She dropped her eyes and began to make the gathered cards into a pack. "It had been weakly from its birth," she said, evading his question.

"Even then," he answered promptly, "it is the saddest thing in the world that a child should die."

"One often hears elderly spinsters say that sort of thing," Emily replied, "but it sounds odd in your mouth."

"I am afraid you think me very ridiculous," he suggested.

"Not exactly ridiculous," she answered. "I think you a little unusual."

"I've had a very rough time," he said, "and the world has knocked me about a bit. I think that it has knocked the nonsense out of me. I only want very simple things now."

"Like simple clothes," Emily added with

a smile, "I'm afraid they cost a great deal of money."

He shook his head. "No," he said, "I want no more than a roof over my head and decent food to eat and a wife and children. That oughtn't to be very hard to get, if you are willing to work for it. And one thing more—I'd like my own people to be fond of me."

Emily had dropped her eyes and was nervously shuffling the pack of cards.

"And for that," he went on, "I don't mind putting up with rotten weather and bad times and sickness and separation and death and still call it good."

Emily laid the cards before her on the table and looked up at him. "You have asked me to marry you, Tom," she said.

He uttered a dry laugh. "Good heavens, I haven't forgotten it," he said.

"Did you ask me because you thought that I would be honest and truthful, a faithful wife and a good mother?"

"Yes," he answered.

An expression of pain passed over her face and her breathing began to come short and quick. "I want to tell you," she began with difficulty, "that since you went away I've been engaged twice."

He looked at her in some surprise, but without grasping the significance which the confession had for her. "Have you?" he said.

"Yes," she answered wretchedly. "It wasn't true when I said that I had waited for you. It wasn't true when I said that I had loved you all the time."

"Why do you tell me this now?" he demanded.

"Because I can't go on with it," she said desperately.

"On with what?" he asked. "What do you mean?"

She rose and went to the fire and, standing with her back to it, faced him. She had recovered her self-possession and spoke in her usual calm, rather cold voice. "I mean this," she said. "I set about to entrap you;

that's the long and the short of it. I set a mean little trap for you and you fell into it, just as I knew you would fall into it. And now I can't go on with it. I haven't sunk that far yet." She stopped, apparently waiting for him to speak, but he said nothing. Tell me what you think of me," she went on, "and bless your stars that you're out of it."

He went to her and put his hands on her shoulders. "You poor girl," he said gently. "You know I believe awfully in the life that I'm going to take you to, even for a woman brought up as you have been. It's a hard life, rather, but it has its points, and I think that after living it a little while the sordidness and the meanness fall away from one."

Her eyes opened wide in amazement. "You're not willing to marry me still!" she exclaimed.

He smiled. "What do you take me for?" he answered.

"But why?" she asked wonderingly.

EMILY IN A NEW LIGHT 195

"Because," he said, "I think we shall be very happy."

Emily shook her head and her eyes filled with tears. "I never expect to be happy," she answered. "You don't know me, Tom. I'm too old to change now."

"I've learned to ask awfully little of people," he said encouragingly.

Emily dried her eyes with her handkerchief, straightened up and in her usual self-contained manner began to speak. "Do you know why I was so desperately anxious to marry you?" she asked. He made no reply. "Well, I've got three hundred pounds of debts," she went on, answering her own question, "and writs are out against me and I haven't a farthing. The mere announcement of my engagement is enough to set me free for the moment. My dressmaker," she added bitterly, "is willing to lend me the money until I'm married."

"Well," said Freeman, "she won't have to, now. I can manage that on my head."

She turned and looked at him as if she found him something impossible to comprehend. "But have you no reproaches for me?" she asked.

Freeman laughed. "I'm rather glad you've made a clean breast of it," he said. "Now we can start fresh and we won't talk of it again."

Emily shook her head. "Do you suppose that I would have humiliated myself like this," she said bitterly, "if I hadn't made up my mind? What would I do on a Rhodesian farm? The only talent I have is for playing bridge."

"You'll be able to beat me at double dummy in the evenings," he answered.

"But you don't understand what I am," she went on. "When I grew desperate and thought it would be easy to catch you, I made up my mind that after we were married, I should get you back to England as soon as I could, and once there, I thought it would be easy to invent excuses to prevent our going out again. You see, I've been

EMILY IN A NEW LIGHT

nothing but heartless and selfish through it all."

"At the same time," he said gently, "you might grow to care for me and then you wouldn't mind staying where I was."

"I?" said Emily. "I care?" She shook her head. "There's no possibility of love for me any more. All the love I'm capable of was wasted years ago."

"Let us risk it at all events," he said. He came towards her and held out his hands, but she backed away.

"No, Tom," she cried desperately, "I can't! I can't! I can't!"

"Why not?" he demanded.

"There is something in me that I didn't know," she answered; "something I don't understand. Perhaps I am a better woman than I thought. I wanted it so much, but now I haven't a spark of love in my heart for you, and I can't do it. It mightn't be so difficult," she went on, "if you loved me, but you don't, do you? Be honest! Real love, I mean."

"It may come," he said.

"No," she answered. "It wouldn't. This is a moment when I am better than I am and I know it. I know what I really am, and what I should be if you married me. You haven't deserved that I should make you unhappy. I can't treat you like that. You've been a perfect brick to me, and I won't be such a cad."

"You know you are talking rather rot," he answered, "aren't you?"

"No," she said firmly. "I'm talking sense. I can't marry you, not only for your sake, but mine. It would be indecent." She turned to the chair over the arm of which her long gloves were lying, picked them up and began to move toward the door. Halfway she stopped and turned around. "Come," she said, "we've been ranting horribly, you and I. I'm sure that we've been making ourselves perfectly ridiculous."

He stood by the fireplace, watching her with a curious smile on his lips. "Well," he said, "it begins to look as if I shall have to go back to Africa without a wife after all."

"Oh, I hope not," said Emily. There was a note of tenderness in her voice that had not been there before. "I hope you'll get a nice, helpful woman to go back with you. And I should like her to be very simple and unspoiled."

"But, my dear," said Freeman, "where the dickens am I to find such a paragon?"

Emily laughed. "I haven't an idea," she said. "Only I hope you do. You deserve it."

There was a pause and then Freeman started up, as if an idea had just come to him. "I have half a mind to marry Smith," he said.

"Don't be silly," she answered with an amused smile.

"But I believe we'd suit one another uncommonly well," said Freeman.

"But you couldn't marry a servant," said Emily.

"That's all rot," said Freeman. "When you are thirty miles from anywhere people aren't ladies and gentlemen, but men and women. And sometimes beasts."

"I suppose that is so," she answered slowly.

"It is undeniably so," he continued, "and they take rank according to what they are, as men and women, not according to what their parents were."

"Are you in love with her?" Emily asked, drawing a step nearer and looking at him seriously.

"If you put a strong, healthy man and a strong, healthy woman together," he replied, "love will come."

"Then why don't you ask her?" she suggested.

"I think I will," said Freeman.

Emily burst into a peal of laughter. "You foolish creature!" she exclaimed. "Still I don't know that it would be any worse to be snapped up by Smith than by me." She had finished putting on her gloves and turned to the table for her purse and bag. "I must be off," she said.

"I say," said Freeman, "what about your three hundred pounds?"

"That's all right," she answered. "I fortunately have my dressmaker's check. I've just got her a new customer, so she won't be more than rather disagreeable when she hears that my fourth engagement is broken off."

He said nothing, but went to the bell and pressed it.

"What are you ringing for?" she asked.

"I thought you were going," he answered. "I wanted the door opened for you."

"Are you so anxious to get rid of me?" she asked chaffingly.

"Of course not," he said; "but weren't you really going?"

"I was going to see Rose," Emily answered. "It would be fatal if she turned you out of the house just now."

"Why?" he asked. "It was bound to come, you know."

"But how could you prosecute your siege of Smith's young heart," she answered, "if you were banished? You must remember, parlour maids have only one evening a week out, and in well-regulated households they are not allowed to receive company without the chaperonage of the cook."

"You think I'm joking," he said seriously, "but I'm not."

"Then I'll certainly go and appease Rose," said Emily. "I have a peculiar knack for persuading people who've had a row that each was in the right and that neither meant a single word of what they said."

"You are very good," he said, "and you can safely tell Rose that I am awfully sorry if I offended her."

"I'll fix it," she said confidently, and turned and went out.

A moment later Smith entered the room and stood standing at attention, as if waiting for an order. Freeman, who had forgotten for the moment that he had rung the bell, looked at her perplexedly.

FREEMAN IS A SECOND TIME REJECTED

CHAPTER XII

FREEMAN IS A SECOND TIME REJECTED

Smith and Freeman stood, gazing at one another. Finally Smith broke the silence. "Did you ring, sir?" she asked.

"No," he answered vaguely.

"The drawing-room indicator went up, sir," said Smith politely but with firmness.

"I lie in my throat," cried Freeman vehemently. "I rang by mistake. I thought Miss Chapman was going away. I'm sorry."

"Very good, sir," said Smith, and she turned to go.

Before she reached the door he called her back. "I wonder," he said hesitatingly, "if you would bring me a small drink?"

"Yes, sir," she answered. "What would you like, sir?"

"I think a little drop of whiskey and soda would exactly fit the case," he suggested.

"Very good, sir," said Smith, and she disappeared.

He had never seen her more professional and parlour-maidish. When she had gone, he dropped into the armchair by the fire and tried to think clearly. Like most strong, self-confident men, convention counted for very little with him. There was even an exhilaration in the prospect of defying it. The difficult question was whether what he proposed to do was fair to the girl, whether as individuals they were really suited to each other and might be expected to work out a useful and happy life together. Without being in love with her, from the physical point of view she attracted him greatly. Her strong, lithe figure and perfect skin were radiant with health and feminine charm. Her eyes and hair any woman might have envied, as well as the double row of regular white teeth, and her large, well-cut mouth. As far as he knew or could judge, her character seemed as exceptional as her physical organisation. Freeman was a believer in what the expression of the human mouth reveals of the individual and, judging by that, Smith's was a fine, high-minded personality with that meekness which, when it is born of strength, is one of the most attractive of feminine qualities. However, his mental debatings were cut short by her return with the tray, on which stood the decanter, glass and soda bottle.

"Thank you," he said. "This is very nice."

"Is that all, sir?" she asked.

He pretended to be busy pouring out the soda and not to hear. She waited for a moment and then started towards the door. "Oh, Smith," he called after her, "what are you doing now?"

She stopped and looked back at him questioningly. "I was just going to decant the claret for dinner, sir," she answered.

"Yes, I see," he said, helping himself rather mechanically to the drink before him.

"I wanted to tell you, that is, I see that you have been having a great game with my clothes."

"Me, sir?" said Smith perplexed.

"You've marked every confounded thing that I have with a large T. F.," he answered.

"I'm sorry, sir," she began, "I thought—"

"Don't think I'm not grateful," he said quickly. "It's awfully jolly of you to have put my things in good order."

"Well, I think they are in reasonably good order now, sir," she assented. "Wherever you go, no one will be able to say you're not decent."

"And that's a very jolly thing to be, isn't it?" he went on.

"Well," said Smith, "some people seem to like going about in rags." She seemed to consider that her duties in the drawing-room were at an end and slowly started again for the door.

He watched her, despairing of making conversation, for she was apparently in an ultra professional mood. "You see, at home," he called after her, "I haven't got anyone to look after me."

This last shot took effect. The statement aroused her interest and the result of their previous and more human conversations was to make it easier for her to be drawn into an expression of personal opinion. "Haven't you got a woman in the house at all, sir?" she exclaimed in surprise.

"Nothing to speak of," he said.

She looked at him and smiled one of her faint, inscrutable, delightful smiles, such a smile as she had indulged in freely with Mr. Fletcher, the janitor, but now properly reduced in size and intensity out of respect to Mrs. Dallas-Baker's drawing-room. "It must be in a state," she observed.

He half pretended to resent the remark. "I don't know about that," he said.

"Well," said Smith, "I always say that a farmhouse wants a mistress. There's something to do from morning till night and a man can't do half what a woman can."

Freeman was too delighted with his success to trust himself to look at her. He sipped his whiskey and soda and answered gravely, "That's entirely a matter of opinion. By the way," he added, "would you like to look at my farm?"

"Yes, sir, I should," she answered simply.

He rose, went to the writing table, and in a moment returned with the surveyor's map of his land.

"Oh!" said Smith, with a shade of disappointment, "I thought you'd got some photographs, sir; I don't know what all that means."

"I'll show you," he said. "Now, look here. That's corn and that's pasture, and there's the river running right through it. It's worth a pot of money, that river. Sweet water for the stock all the year around. And look at that little blue square there; that's my house, and not a half bad house, either."

"I shouldn't like to look in the corners," said Smith demurely. "I expect there's a lot of dust and dirt in them."

Their heads had been close together, as

they bent over the map, and the thin, clean fragrance of her hair came to him and made his pulses throb. Suddenly she looked up and stepped back, feeling his eyes fixed upon her.

"Hello," said Freeman, "why are you blushing?"

"I'm not blushing," said Smith, with spirit; "but it makes me uncomfortable when you stare at me."

Freeman looked at her with mock gravity. "What's your health like?" he demanded.

"My health?" she answered vaguely. "I don't know; I never think about it."

"That looks as if you hadn't much to complain about," he observed.

"Servants, you know, sir," she went on, "can't afford to make a fuss every time they have a finger ache."

"Ever ill in bed?" he asked.

"Not since I was quite a little tot, sir," she replied. Her face showed her surprise at his questions, but he went on without satisfying it.

"Can you cook?" he asked.

"You do ask me funny questions," she said, at last.

"Not at all," he said severely. "It's a very reasonable question. If you're thinking of going to New South Wales, it's most important that you should be able to cook. What do you think would be the use of having a good hand with silver out there?"

She said nothing for a moment and seemed to be trying to recall something to mind. Finally she spoke: "Was the dinner you had on Friday all right, sir?" she asked.

"I quite forget," he answered.

Smith smiled again. "I expect it was, or else you would have noticed it," she said. "Men are always the same. If things go right, they don't notice anything; but if there's the smallest thing wrong, they grumble for a week."

"Oh!" he exclaimed reproachfully, "I think that's putting it rather strong. Women are much more exacting than men."

"Well, it's my experience, sir," she replied.

"But what about the dinner on Friday?" he demanded.

"Nothing, sir," she answered; "only cook had one of her sick headaches, and I did it."

"You don't have sick headaches, do you?" he asked.

Smith laughed outright at this. "Me, sir?" she said. "I've never had a sick headache in my life."

He looked at her admiringly, but maintained his mock-serious, rather fault-finding expression. "I dare say you can do fal-lalla and fancy things," he began. He saw that she was puzzled, and explained. "I was going back to Friday's dinner," he said.

"You do jump about so, sir!" she said rather hopelessly.

"I suppose I do," he answered, "but the point is, can you do good, honest, English cooking?"

"When mother wasn't well, I cooked for thirteen often and often at home," she replied. Her manner was simple and respectful, as it invariably was, but there was a faint note of scorn in her voice that delighted Freeman.

"Were you happy at home?" he asked.

"Oh, yes, sir," she answered. "I like a farm. I wouldn't ever have come away, if there hadn't been so many of us."

Freeman was silent a moment. He was weighing the pros and cons for the last time and with as much deliberation as he ever gave to his personal affairs. "I don't know why you are so particularly struck on New South Wales," he said at length.

"Well, you see, sir," she answered, "I've got my sister there."

"I suppose that is a reason," he said. "However, I wonder if you would like Rhodesia? It's a jolly climate and the country's coming on like anything. You'd be very useful on my farm."

"Well, sir," she answered, "I couldn't very well come to you, when there's no lady in the house, could I?"

AGAIN REJECTED

She took the empty glass from the card table, where he had placed it, and put it on the tray. "Shall I take the whiskey away, sir?" she asked.

He nodded. But as she turned to go he stopped her and, in a matter-of-fact tone, as if he were inquiring the day of the month, said: "Will you marry me?"

Smith turned on him with a face blazing with indignation. "Me, sir?" she said, stiffly.

"Yes," he said, "you, Smith. By the way, what is your name?"

"Smith, sir," she answered shortly.

"I meant your Christian name," he explained.

She looked at him with a quiet dignity that admitted no evasion. "I prefer to be called Smith, sir," she replied.

But Freeman was not to be snubbed. "Why?" he demanded.

"In the houses that I've been used to," she answered, "the servants have always been called by their surnames, except the footmen." She picked up the tray and started for the door.

Without seeming to threaten her or bar her passage, he placed himself before it. "Where are you going?" he asked.

"I was going to decant the claret, sir," she answered. "The master likes it to stand before dinner."

"I see," said Freeman politely, "but has it slipped your memory that I asked you a question?"

She looked him steadily in the eyes. "You were only laughing at me, sir," she said.

"I beg your pardon," he said earnestly; "I was doing nothing of the kind. I was very much in earnest." He broke off, noticing a look of perplexity on her face that apparently had nothing to do with the question that he was asking to have answered. "What's the matter, now?" he demanded.

"I was wondering, sir," she answered demurely, "how I was going to get through that door with you standing in front of it."

He took the tray from her with gentle

firmness and put it on the table. Then he planted himself before her. "Now," he said, "I am certainly not going to let you get out of the room till you've answered me. Hang it all, you don't get a serious proposal of marriage every day. You might give it serious attention."

Smith stiffened herself and took a step as if she would pass him. "Thank you very much, sir," she said with dignity, "but I don't think it would do."

"What?" he said in amazement; "not do? And why not?"

"Well, sir," she answered, "for one thing, I'm a domestic servant and you're a gentleman."

"Oh, no; I'm not," he answered quickly. "I've long given up that delusion. I'll grant you I *was* a gentleman," he went on. "I used to hunt and buy my clothes in Saville Row; I belonged to three clubs, and used to take chorus girls to supper at the Savoy; but I'm not a gentleman, now."

His earnestness had a curious effect upon

Smith. "Oh, yes, you are, sir," she said insistently. "I knew it the moment I saw you."

"Don't be so disagreeable," said Freeman. "I ought to know. And I wish you wouldn't call me 'sir' every other minute. It does put one off, when one is making a proposal of marriage."

Smith looked at him, uncertain whether to smile or not. "I think I know my place, sir," she said gravely, and made a movement to take the tray again, but again he checked her.

"I suppose you think I have forgotten mine," he suggested.

"It's not for me to say, sir," she replied meekly, but with a sparkle in her eyes.

He smiled. "Well, that's proof positive that I'm not a gentleman," he said.

Smith, feeling herself defeated at dialectic, shifted her ground. "I don't hold with people marrying out of their proper station," she said. "I've never seen any good come of it."

"I wish you wouldn't make general reflections," he replied. "What I want is a straightforward answer."

"I thought I gave it to you, sir," she said quietly.

Freeman made a grimace and winced. "It wasn't the right one," he said. "I think you had better try again."

She shook her head slowly. "It wouldn't be right," she said. Then, as if asking herself a question, she added half aloud, "What would the mistress say?"

Freeman smiled. "I dare say her observations would be a little pointed," he answered; "but you know hard words break no bones." She bent down for a third time to lift the tray with the decanter and a third time he stopped her. "Come, my dear," he said, "don't let's talk nonsense. You'll make me a very good wife, and I'll try to make you a good husband. I've got a comfortable home to take you to, and you'll be your own mistress, which is much better than being in service."

She smiled, as if inwardly amused. "That's what Fletcher said only last week," she observed.

"Fletcher?" he exclaimed, with well-feigned surprise. "Who the dickens is Fletcher?"

"He's the porter, sir," she answered.

"And has he been making you a proposal of marriage?" he demanded.

"Yes, sir," she said simply.

"Well, I'll be hanged!" Freeman exclaimed. "And what did you say to him?"

"I didn't say yes and I didn't say no," Smith replied.

"I see," said Freeman, "you're keeping him dangling."

"I can't make up my mind," she replied.

"You made up your mind about me jolly quick," he said, with an aggrieved air.

"Oh, well, sir," she answered, "you're different. He's very much more suitable."

"That's flattering," said Freeman grimly.

"I don't mean it rudely," said Smith; "but

when I marry, I want to marry a workingman."

Freeman laughed aloud. "God bless my soul!" he exclaimed. "What do you suppose I am? I bet you, I do more work in a day than half a dozen Fletchers in a week."

"Brain work," said Smith, with calm assurance. "I don't count that."

"Not a bit of it," he went on indignantly. "Manual labour, my child."

"Oh, I know what gentlemen call manual labour," Smith replied firmly, "looking on while people they pay wages do the work."

"You know I shall slap you in a minute," said Freeman, with a laugh.

Even his pleasantry did not recall Smith to an immediate sense of her professional self. Her contempt for amateur manual labourers was too deep and, once stirred, it was bound to find expression. "I've seen gentlemen farmers at work," she said. "You know what we say about them down our way? 'Neither gentlemen nor farmers.'"

Freeman laughed again. "That's kind

of you, I'm sure," he said. "But in South Africa things are very different."

"I didn't mean to apply it to you, sir," she said hastily and in some alarm.

"That's all right," he answered. "What I want to find out is what you want in a husband?"

"Me, sir?" she asked in some surprise.

"Yes, you," he replied. "I suppose you know."

Smith thought a moment. "Well, I wouldn't have a lazy man," she began.

"Please note," he put in, "that I'm up a good hour before anybody else in this house."

"I don't say you're not an early riser," she assented.

"Well, that's in my favour, to begin with," he said.

"It's a great bother," she said, "when I want to do the drawing-room every morning to find you sitting in it at half-past seven."

"We'll pass that by," he suggested. "What else do you want in a husband?"

"Well," she answered, "I want a man who's got a strong pair of arms. The way I look on it is this: One never knows what's going to happen. A man may be thrown out of work, but if he's not above putting his hand to anything, and he's got a strong pair of arms, he won't starve in England or anywhere else."

"That is quite true," said Freeman, "and now I invite you to feel my muscle." He doubled up his biceps and Smith touched it lightly with her fingers.

"Oh, yes," she said, "it's gentleman's strength. I know that. It's all very well for playing games with, but when it comes to useful things, to carrying a heavy box up five flights of stairs—"

He interrupted her with a triumphant laugh. "My dear child," he said, "I was luggage porter for six months in the best hotel in Johannesburg."

Smith looked at him in open astonishment. "You, sir?" she exclaimed.

"Yes, I," he answered, "and glad to get

it, too. That's one in the eye for Fletcher, isn't it?"

Smith tossed her head slightly. "Fletcher's very wiry and willing," she said in reply. "He says he can bend an iron bar with his hands, and I shouldn't be surprised if it was true."

"I would," said Freeman ungenerously. "More than that, I don't see much good in being able to bend an iron bar with one's hands."

Smith considered the matter for a moment. "Neither do I, sir," she said conscientiously, "but it looks well."

"No," he said, shaking his head, "too showy for my taste."

She made no reply, but, picking up her tray, started for the door. He was still standing in her path and she stopped when she reached him and dropped her eyes. "You won't take it amiss my having said 'no' to you, sir?" she asked shyly.

"Not a bit," he said; "it's the fortune of war."

"You see," she went on, "one has to think of one's self in these matters, doesn't one?"

"I, for one, do," he answered.

"And now, sir, if you please, may I go and decant the wine for dinner?" she pleaded.

"You may," he said. Then a flash of reckless fun woke in him and he stepped in front of her again. "Won't you give me a kiss?" he asked. He waited for her answer, wondering whether the lightnings of her just indignation would consume him utterly. He was prepared even for bodily violence. To his surprise, she looked him quietly in the eyes and said: "If it will give you any pleasure, sir."

"Upon my word!" he exclaimed, "you're such a sensible girl, it quite takes my breath away! Anyone else would have made no end of fuss about my impudence!"

Smith smiled demurely. "Oh, well, sir," she said, "what I say is, no great harm's done by a kiss." She put her cheek out, as if in a spirit of bravado, and he kissed it.

"Well, I'm dashed!" he exclaimed, and she disappeared through the doorway.

Freeman was somewhat roughly awakened from contemplating the sensation which Smith's original course of action had aroused in him by the entrance of Mr. Peppercorn. The youth had his hat on the back of his head and seemed warm, out of breath and in a hurry.

"Where's Rose?" he demanded.

"I think she is in her room," said Freeman, "with Miss Chapman."

"Oh!" said Mr. Peppercorn. He thought a moment, then went to the door and called down the passage. "I say, Smith, tell Mrs. Dallas-Baker I'm here." Then he came back and dropped into his favourite chair. "Freeman!" he exclaimed, "I am a hero! Upon my soul, I am!"

"Unquestionably you behaved with great nobility," said Freeman laughing.

"I did," said Peppercorn. "And I suppose you have been havin' hysterics, what?"

"I averted that catastrophe," Freeman

answered, "by the application of a small whiskey and soda." He broke off as Rose pushed the door open and came in, followed by Emily Chapman. She glanced at her brother without any great affection, but in a manner that evidently indicated that Emily's efforts at peace-making had been successful.

"Well?" she said, addressing Peppercorn.

"Well," he answered, "I took her home according to orders."

"Was she much upset?" Emily asked.

"She did seem a bit put out, don't you know," replied Mr. Peppercorn. "She kept on saying, 'What will Otto say?'"

"Silly little fool!" Rose exclaimed. "She's frightened to death of Otto."

"She is," said Mr. Peppercorn. "But then he makes himself awfully unpleasant. I suppose he'll make a regular fuss about this!"

"I suppose so," said Rose. "He's dreadfully common."

"It *will* be very vulgar of him, won't it,"

said Freeman gravely, "if he is annoyed at his baby's death?"

Rose shot him a look, but what she had in mind to say she left unsaid, for Smith entered the room.

"If you please, ma'am," she said, "I can't draw the cork of the claret the master put out for dinner."

"Then you had better ask Fletcher to do it," said Rose.

"Fletcher was in the kitchen, ma'am," Smith replied. "He's tried already."

"Do you mean to say that Fletcher can't draw a cork?" said Freeman. "I thought he was a kind of young Hercules."

"Well, sir," said Smith, "if he can't draw it, nobody can."

"Bring the bottle," he answered, "and let me have a shot."

"Very well, sir," she said, and went out.

"I wish I could stop on," said Emily Chapman, "and see the end of the cork, but I must be going. Good-bye, Rose, dear."

"Good-bye," Rose answered. "Please forgive these domestic details."

"I like them," said Emily. "Smith looks upon me as a member of the family." She held out her hand to Freeman. "Good-bye and good luck," she said.

"Thank you," he answered; "thank you very much."

It may have been something in Freeman's tone or in his manner that excited Mr. Peppercorn's lively sense of curiosity. At all events, his eyes lit up. "What are you wishing him good luck in?" he demanded.

Emily smiled. "His matrimonial schemes," she replied.

"Like those of mice and men," Freeman observed, "they 'gang oft agley.'"

"My dear fellow," said Mr. Peppercorn, "don't talk Scotch to us. You should take my advice and put an advertisement in the *Telegraph*."

"I'm beginning to think that I shall be driven to it," said Freeman.

"Good-bye again," said Emily, and she waved her hand at Freeman and went out arm in arm with Rose.

In a moment Smith returned with the bottle of claret. "Fletcher's had another try at it, sir, and he can't move it," she said. "Is there any use of your trying?"

"Fletcher's a donkey," said Freeman. He took the bottle from her and, gripping it between his knees, made a mighty effort, but the cork never budged.

Smith watched him with an air of polite disinterestedness, but beneath the professional Smith, Freeman knew that Smith, the woman, was sitting in judgment upon him. The veins in his head began to swell, but the cork withstood him.

"I'm afraid you'll strain yourself, sir," she said politely. She dropped her eyes, but the faint glimmer of a smile was on her lips.

"Shut up!" he exclaimed wrathfully and, throwing every pound of himself into the effort, the refractory cork slowly began to come and left the bottle with a little pop.

"I'm afraid you'll strain yourself, Sir," she said politely.

"Upon my soul," exclaimed Algy, admiringly, "you *are* a strong beast!"

Freeman handed the bottle to Smith, who looked at him without expression, and then gravely untwisted the cork from the corkscrew. "You can give the cork to Fletcher with my compliments," he said. "Perhaps he'd like to wear it on his watch chain."

Without making any response, except a whispered "Thank you, sir," she turned and left the room.

CHAPTER XIII

SMITH AND FREEMAN CONTINUE DISCUSSION

For five days, peace, if not good will, reigned in the Dallas-Baker abode. Rose treated her brother with at least outward civility and, on his part, Tom took pains to refrain from criticising her or interfering in any way with the life of the household. During this time he saw Smith only as she served him at meals or as he met her about the house. He avoided scrupulously any conversation that might embarrass her or put her at a disadvantage. Emily Chapman he did not see at all. Since the day that he had been refused both by her and Smith she had avoided Credinton Court. However, he had received a note from her, for that evening, after she had gone, he had written a check for three hundred pounds and had sent it to her. Her gratitude had been deep and sincere, but she had shown no symptoms of changing her mind as regards her determination not to marry him. And when Freeman was honest with himself, he not only gave her the credit of acting upon high motives, but he congratulated himself upon an escape. As a matter of fact, since Smith had refused him, he had begun to regard her in a wholly different light. It was not that he merely wanted to get married, but that he wanted to marry *her*. As well as he could judge in his saner and better ordered moments, he was in love. But no fairy princess, or flesh and blood royalty seemed farther away and more impossible of attainment than Smith. "For, after all," as he thought it out to himself, "one can with decency try to scale a fairy princess's tower or elope with the daughter of a royal highness, yet it is quite impossible to annoy a parlour maid with attentions which she does not care to encourage." So he decided to grin and bear it, as he had grinned and borne many things before and as his philosophy of life prescribed.

One rainy Sunday morning he was lying on the window seat in the drawing-room with a book, which he pretended to read. His perusal of the page had become a pretence, when Smith came in with a tray on which were half-a-dozen vases of fresh flowers. She deposited the tray on the table and was disposing the vases about the room as her sense of æsthetic fitness determined. The last bowl of roses evidently troubled her, for she tried it in various positions and, after each new experiment, withdrew to the middle of the room to witness and weigh the effect.

The fourth time that the bowl underwent a removal, Freeman looked up from his book and smiled. "They were all right before," he said quietly, "don't you think so?"

Smith started and turned toward him. "You did give me a shock, sir!" she said naïvely. "I thought you were reading."

"When you came in, I suddenly discovered that I had something better to do," he replied.

She made no answer, but set the roses on the piano top, and Freeman went on: "It may interest you to know that I am going away next week."

"We shall be sorry to lose you, sir," she answered respectfully.

"Thank you," he said drily; "but I can't flatter myself that it will disturb your night's rest."

"It would take a lot to do that," she said. Her manner was so perfect that he was unable to decide whether there was irony in her remark or not. He suspected that there was, having become familiar with the humorous possibilities of the human underlying Smith; but she shielded herself so completely behind the parlour maid that he had no point of attack open to him.

"Is there anything else, sir?" she added.

"Nothing, thank you," he answered.

She started for the door with her tray and then, obeying a sudden impulse, turned about and came towards him. "Excuse me, sir," she said, and hesitated.

"Yes?" he replied encouragingly.

"I wanted to thank you for being so kind to me, sir," she said shyly.

"That's very good of you," he answered. "I've not noticed that I've been particularly kind."

"You have," said Smith. "Many gentlemen would have taken advantage of—of what you said last week to be familiar."

"I could hardly look upon it as encouragement to be familiar when you refused to marry me," he replied.

"Or you might have been short with me," she went on. "I know it's silly, when you are in a situation, but I don't like it when people talk to you as if you were a dog."

"Now you are being idiotic," said Freeman. "You'd better get on with your work."

"Yes, sir," she said and turned away, but before she had reached the door he called her back.

"Just a moment," he said. "It never

struck me that I might be making it rather uncomfortable for you here."

"Well," Smith answered frankly, "it isn't your fault, sir; but cook says she thinks I ought to give notice."

Freeman laughed drily. "So you have discussed it with cook?" he said.

"You don't mind, sir, do you?" she asked anxiously.

"Not a bit," he answered. "You can discuss it with the dustman, if you like."

"Well, sir," she went on, "mother asked cook to keep an eye on me, so I thought I had better tell her what you said. Though the fact is," she added, "I keep more of an eye on cook."

"Do you?" asked Freeman with an amused smile.

"Yes," said Smith. "It seems to me that single women, when they get near forty, always become rather silly about men."

Freeman chuckled. "And what did you say to cook when she advised you to leave?" he asked.

"I said I didn't know how she'd manage without me," Smith answered frankly.

Freeman threw his head back and laughed, but Smith's gravity remained undisturbed.

"I see that you have a proper opinion of yourself," he said.

"Well, it's not everyone who could get on with cook, sir," she answered, "so I thought I'd wait a week and see what happened."

"On cook's account?" he suggested.

"Yes, sir," said Smith.

"Well, I hope I haven't made myself very objectionable," he observed gravely.

"No, sir," she said, "that's what I wanted to thank you for. You've been just the same as you were before, except—" she added with a note of regret in her voice—"that you used to chat a little with me now and then, and you haven't said a word to me until to-day."

"I've thought a good deal," he said gravely.

She looked at him, perplexed. "Have you, sir?" she said.

"Yes," he answered. "I have thought a good deal about you and I think you are a very good girl and that the man who marries you will be a devilish lucky chap. And I hope," he added, "that he will be as good to you as you deserve."

Smith smiled her charming, frank smile. "I hope he'll be better than that, sir," she answered.

"Well, don't let him know that such a thing is possible," said Freeman. He picked up his book feeling that he had said all that he had a right to say and feeling too, that he was drifting rapidly into dangerous waters.

He fixed his eyes upon the page and held them there, expecting to hear her as she turned the handle of the door and catch a parting look at her as she went out. But the door handle was not turned and he looked up a moment later to find her standing somewhat nearer him than she had been with an expression of shy and troubled concern on her face.

As he caught her eye, she looked down. "You didn't care the other day," she began with evident difficulty, "when I said 'no,' did you, sir?"

Freeman was silent for a moment. Then he sat up and put his feet to the floor.

"No, curiously enough," he said huskily, "but, Smith, I care now."

She raised her eyes, looked at him steadily and then dropped them again.

"I suppose that I am like a lot of people," he went on, getting more control of himself as he proceeded. "I don't really want a thing till I can't get it. It's very silly, isn't it? I asked you to marry me, well, because I wanted a wife and rather admired you, and you seemed to be on the spot. I fell in love with you the minute you refused to marry me."

"I don't believe if anyone was really in love," said Smith quietly, "they could make jokes about it."

"That's what we all think when we are very young," he answered. "When we get older, we know that circumstances alter cases, and we find out, too, that making jokes about things that are very near us doesn't mean that we don't feel. Rather the opposite."

"I don't think I understand that," said Smith.

"Well, suppose a man was very shy," said Freeman. "Suppose he felt so deeply that he couldn't speak seriously about the things that were of first importance to him; well, joking about them might seem the best way out of it."

"I can't make you out, sir," said Smith simply.

"I wonder if it would change your opinion about me, if you could?" he answered.

"I don't know," she said. "And no matter what I thought of you, sir, all the things that I said were objections would be just as true, wouldn't they, sir?"

"Yes, and no," he replied. "When people care for one another, I suspect that objections, no matter how logical, don't seem objections any longer. There always seems a way around them. Don't you think so?"

"I don't know," she answered. "I never—" she stopped, for a bell rang violently in the passage.

"Is that the telephone?" he asked.

"It's the front door, sir," she answered. "I expect it's Mr. Peppercorn."

"Hadn't you better let him in?" he suggested, suddenly coming to a realising sense of things. He opened his book and took his place on the window seat again.

CHAPTER XIV

EMILY MAKES NEW PLANS

FREEMAN, ensconced on the window seat, had read hardly more than a single sentence, when the door opened again and Smith announced Miss Chapman. He sprang up, tossed the book aside, and went toward her. "You're quite a stranger," he said.

"How do you do?" said Emily, and extended her hand.

"It's at least a century since you were here," he insisted gallantly.

"Five days, to be precise," she answered.

"Well, have it your own way," he said. "I am afraid that Rose is not in," he went on. "Providence having sent us a wet Sunday, Rose thought she'd get even with Providence by taking Herbert to church."

"I didn't come to see Rose," Emily replied, "and I came at this time because I thought that I might catch you alone."

He looked at her, mystified. "That's very flattering to a man of my age," he observed.

"I wanted to thank you," she said gravely and with more feeling than her voice usually showed.

"Good Heavens! what for?" he exclaimed.

"Tom," she said, "it *was* good of you to send me that three hundred pounds!"

"But you can't bring that up against me again," he protested. "You've written the most ample thanks. In fact, I'm overcome and mortified already."

"You don't know what it means," she went on, after a pause. "I've paid my dressmaker. For the first time in my life I haven't a debt in the world—except to you."

"You must feel immensely relieved," he said kindly.

She laughed. "Just at present," she said, "I feel rather lonely."

EMILY MAKES NEW PLANS 251

"You'll get used to it," he answered.

"But I've done something else," she continued, lowering her voice confidentially. "I've sold everything I possessed."

"But why?" he asked in surprise.

"I'm going away," she answered.

He looked at her, not understanding quite what she meant. "Are you, indeed?" he said politely.

"Yes," said Emily, "I've come to say good-bye to you all, and I wanted to tell you what I'm going to do, because you've had a good deal to do with it. I hope you won't think it's awfully silly of me," she added.

"I have no doubt I shall," he observed.

Emily smiled gaily. "You know," she began, "I really did rather a good action when I refused to marry you. Neither of us cared two straws for the other and it would have been all to my advantage. But I'm glad I released you. I don't know just why I did it. It was something stronger than myself, that just took me and made me. But it was madness——" She paused and laughed. "Good actions are like drug taking—the first step may lead you, goodness knows, where."

He looked at her, in comic alarm. "You fill me with consternation," he said.

"I felt desperately virtuous, afterwards," she went on, "and I had a sleepless night or two and I cried a good deal."

"I say," Freeman exclaimed earnestly, "I am awfully sorry!"

"There is no need to be," she answered, "because I was quite happy. I don't know what came over me. I suddenly felt so horribly worthless and I began to hate the life I've been leading for the past ten years."

He looked at her sympathetically. "I expect you've had rather a rotten time," he said.

"Rather," she assented. "Well, when I began to wonder where I was drifting, I looked at myself in the glass and shuddered. I'm only thirty, and I'm a painted harridan already. 'What shall I be in ten years?' I

EMILY MAKES NEW PLANS

thought. I've had enough of that sort of thing, I decided, so I began next morning by washing my face."

"As an economy or as a symbol?" Freeman asked.

Emily laughed. "Both," she answered. "Then it seemed that I had wasted so much time that I must try and make amends for it by up and doing something at once towards earning an honest living. I told you the other day that the only talent I had was for playing bridge. I grossly misled you. I'm really not at all a bad cook."

"By Jove!" exclaimed Freeman, in amazement.

"It's so," she said. "Perhaps you remember telling me that Smith was thinking of emigrating to New South Wales? Well, I made inquiries."

"You?" exclaimed Freeman, again.

"Yes, I," said Emily, "and I've got a second class ticket in my pocket for which I haven't had to pay anything. I start for Sydney at once, and on my arrival I'm guaranteed a place at quite a decent salary."

Freeman gazed at her in open-mouthed amazement. "But do you know what you are in for?" he said. "I think it's awfully brave of you."

"It isn't a bit," she replied calmly. "It's merely the least of a number of evils."

She stopped, and they both listened, for they heard the sound of a key in the front door, and then of the door opening.

"It's Rose and Herbert," said Freeman.

"You needn't tell them what I am going to do," she said hurriedly. "They wouldn't understand."

Freeman nodded assent and Rose came in.

"Oh, Emily dear!" she exclaimed with an amiable enthusiasm, "I've been wondering what on earth had become of you!"

Emily extended a cheek and the two women kissed one another in a perfunctory way.

"I've been very busy," said Emily, in answer to Rose's question. "I've had a number of important things to do and to decide about."

"Really?" said Rose vaguely. She glanced about the room and a shadow crossed her face. "Isn't Algy here?" she asked.

"I've not seen him," said Freeman.

"How tiresome he is!" Rose exclaimed.

"I've no doubt he'll turn up in time for lunch," Freeman remarked reassuringly.

Rose sat down stiffly and began taking off her gloves. "I'm beginning to think," she said icily, "that he's making too great a convenience of us."

Freeman raised his eyebrows and looked at Dallas-Baker, who had followed his wife into the room.

"I'm afraid Rose isn't in a very good humour this morning," he said regretfully. "I wish Algy would come."

"Do you really?" said Freeman

"I do, indeed," Dallas-Baker replied with emphasis, "and I hope he's not going to be late for luncheon. It always puts Rose out to be kept waiting."

"Perhaps he won't come at all," Freeman suggested. "As it was raining and you couldn't play golf, I daresay he thought he'd take a day off."

Rose turned to Emily, apparently as much from a desire to change the conversation as to be hospitable and invited her to stay to lunch.

"It's very kind of you," Emily replied, "but I'm afraid I can't."

Rose looked vexed, but she only said: "I'm sorry," in a tone that was anything but regretful, and asked Emily if she had seen Cynthia Rosenberg lately.

"No," Emily replied. "I called, but she wasn't at home."

"I'm very angry with her," said Rose vigorously. "I called twice and I happen to know she was in each time and they wouldn't let me up. I wrote and asked her if I might go and see her, and she hasn't answered my letter."

EMILY MAKES NEW PLANS 257

"I daresay she was very much upset by the baby's death," Dallas-Baker remarked soothingly.

Rose turned on him. "Nonsense!" she said brusquely.

"Well," he replied mildly, "one never can tell how people are going to take these things. She may think that it was a little our fault that she didn't get home in time."

"Oh, Herbert!" Rose exclaimed, "don't begin on that again. I think you're growing more and more prosy every day."

"I've been very much worried by the whole thing," he replied with more firmness than he generally showed. "It was unpleasant. No one can deny that it was unpleasant."

"My dear Herbert," said Rose, "it's ancient history now."

"I'm a great believer in looking facts in the face," he continued, undeterred by her interruption, "and the fact is that people might say very disagreeable things if they knew that—"

"It's quite indifferent to me what people say about me!" Rose exclaimed, taking the words out of her husband's mouth.

While she was still speaking the door had opened softly and Mr. Peppercorn entered. "How lucky I am," he said, coming forward and shaking hands; "I've arrived in the nick of time for a domestic tiff."

"You're very late, my friend," said Rose severely.

"Am I?" said Mr. Peppercorn.

"You know you are," said Rose. "Don't you think you might at least pretend some regret?"

"I precipitate myself at your feet and kiss the hem of your garment," he answered. His remark was in his usual vein of lightness and flippancy, but there seemed to be something laboured about it.

"I am beginning to think that you are growing stupid, Algy," said Rose.

Mr. Peppercorn looked at her shrewdly. "I've noticed you've been thinking that for some time," he said quietly.

Dallas-Baker laughed and shook a warning finger at him. "What happened to you last night, young man?" he said with mock severity. "It was too bad of you to telephone five minutes before dinner that you were unable to come."

"Yes," said Rose coolly, "I've been wondering when it would occur to you to apologise for putting us to inconvenience."

Mr. Peppercorn slowly took out his pocket handkerchief, a corner of which was knotted. "There," he said, pointing to the knot, "look at that. I thought of a most convincing excuse, as I came along, and so that I shouldn't forget it, I tied a knot in my handkerchief. And now it's gone." He shook his head sadly. "I shall never trust a knot in my handkerchief again."

Dallas-Baker laughed, but Rose heard him through without a smile. She was about to speak when Smith appeared in the doorway and announced Mrs. Rosenberg.

A moment later Cynthia's slim figure, dressed in heavy mourning, stood on the threshold of the room, hesitating, apparently, about entering.

"Cynthia?" said Rose in some surprise.

"I didn't expect to find so many people," Mrs. Rosenberg replied, and advanced timidly. "I thought, as it was Sunday—"

Rose went to meet her and kissed her with a show of affection. "What on earth is the matter?" she asked. "What has happened to you? Why wouldn't you see me the other day, when I called?"

Cynthia made no answer at first to Rose's question, because Dallas-Baker had approached her, offered his hand and was expressing his pleasure at seeing her. "I'm glad to have this opportunity of expressing my sympathy with your great loss," he said with some uneasiness.

Rose shot him a look. "Really, Herbert!" she said sharply.

But Mrs. Rosenberg smiled rather mournfully. "It's very kind of you," she said. "I came in for a moment," she went on, "because I had something to say to Rose."

EMILY MAKES NEW PLANS 261

"Would you like us to leave you?" suggested Freeman quickly.

"No, don't bother," she answered.

"Then won't you sit down?" he suggested.

She shook her head. "No, thank you," she said; "I can only stay a minute." She turned to Rose. "You wrote me the other day, Rose," she began.

"Yes," said Rose, "and I've been wondering why on earth you didn't answer."

"Otto wanted me to answer by letter," Cynthia replied, "but I felt I couldn't—I thought I could explain so much better if I saw you." She hesitated, evidently much embarrassed. "It's very difficult."

"You're extraordinarily mysterious!" said Rose. "I simply wrote to ask you when I could come and see you. It was mere politeness."

"I'm afraid I can't ask you to come and see me just yet," Mrs. Rosenberg replied. "You must forgive me. I feel very badly—"

"But why on earth not?" exclaimed Rose.

"Oh, I've had such an awful week!" Cynthia broke out hysterically. "When I got home and the baby was dead, Otto was furious with me. I thought he was going to kill me!"

"The brute!" said Rose.

"I didn't mind that," she went on brokenly. "But he wouldn't speak to me. I had to go to Rachel and ask her to go to him. He said I had married him for his money and was a worthless wife and a worthless mother."

"You oughtn't to have let him talk that way to you," said Rose severely.

"It was true," said Cynthia, dropping her eyes.

"Fortunately," Rose answered, "we don't live in a world where people habitually speak the truth."

"He talked of separating," Mrs. Rosenberg continued, "and I was horribly frightened. It seemed to me as if the whole world were coming to an end."

"Because Otto Rosenberg suggested a separation?" Rose asked ironically.

"I suppose I cared for him more than I knew," she answered. "But at last he said that if I would promise to be more decent, he'd let me stay. And I," she added falteringly, "I promised to give up seeing you."

"Me?" exclaimed Rose in angry amazement.

"All of you," said Mrs. Rosenberg simply—"the people that I have been going about with. He thinks that you are—" she stopped and then added miserably,—"I don't quite know how to put it."

"My dear," said Rose insolently, "you need not trouble to explain. We shall bear the loss of your society with fortitude."

A look of pain crossed Cynthia's pale face. "Don't be too angry with me," she said appealingly. "I felt that I must explain, so that you shouldn't think too badly of me."

"I think you've behaved very pluckily," said Freeman.

Mrs. Rosenberg thanked him with her eyes, but said nothing. A moment later she turned to Emily, who was standing by with a smile of half-amused indifference. "I'm afraid it applies to you, also, Emily," she said regretfully.

"Oh, my dear," Emily answered, "don't be troubled about me. I couldn't have seen much more of you in any case. I'm going away."

Rose turned toward her with a quick suspicion and then glanced at Tom. "You going away?" she exclaimed.

"Yes," said Emily with a quiet smile. "I came to say good-bye to you, too. I am going to Australia."

"Australia?" repeated Rose, wonderingly, and again she looked at Tom.

"Yes, Australia," Emily said again. "We shall never battle with one another at bridge again, Rose, dear; at least not for a long time."

EMILY MAKES NEW PLANS

"That will at least be an advantage to my pocket," said Rose with a cold smile.

"I wish you a great deal of good luck, Emily," said Mrs. Rosenberg. "Good-bye." She kissed her on the cheek and then turned to Rose. "Good-bye, Rose. I must be off."

Rose nodded stiffly. "You can tell Otto with my compliments," she began, but stopped, as Freeman interrupted her.

"I wouldn't say anything disagreeable, Rose," he said. "I'm sorry, Mrs. Rosenberg, that I don't know your husband."

"You called him a fat old German when you first came," Mrs. Rosenberg observed with a faint smile.

"I knew him much less than I do now," Freeman replied quickly. "Good-bye." He held out his hand and she took it warmly.

Then Mrs. Rosenberg bowed stiffly to the room in general and, Dallas-Baker holding open the door for her, she took her leave.

When she had gone, Rose burst into a

hard little laugh. "I never heard anything so vulgar and absurd!" she exclaimed. "Did you?"

"I daresay that we shall be able to do without her, my dear," said her husband pompously. "I don't think that either she or her husband were quite our form."

"Still," said Rose bitterly, "we might have discovered that before they turned their back on us."

"That is true," said Dallas-Baker calmly. He looked at his watch. "I've got just time to read a brief before luncheon," he said. "I shall go and put on a smoking jacket. I think my frock coat is growing a little tight for me."

He turned to go, but Emily stopped him. "I'd better say good-bye to you," she said, "for I shall be off in a few minutes."

"Good-bye," he said in his best manner. "I am sure I hope that you will have a pleasant journey," and he went out.

Mr. Peppercorn, who had begun to feel the atmosphere grow kindlier and more pro-

EMILY MAKES NEW PLANS

pitious as regards himself, dropped into a chair and began hunting through his pockets for his cigarette case. "You won't forget to write us, will you, Emily," he said amiably, "and tell us all about the kangaroos?"

"I won't forget," she said, "and I will write you."

"To me," said Rose, with a knowing look, "it is somewhat of a surprise that your destination is Australia. I suppose it is a case of leading the horse to water, but being unable to make him drink."

Emily nodded good-naturedly and shot a glance at Freeman, intended to make him keep silent, for a frown had gathered on his brows and he looked ready to blurt out one of his lectures which so exasperated Rose. "Yes," she said, "it's Australia for lack of the wherewithal to make it Paris." The two women kissed, said good-bye, and separated.

"Truly an affecting leave-taking!" observed Mr. Peppercorn, carefully selecting a cigarette as was his custom, although they were all the same brand.

"Very," said Emily.

Freeman crossed to her and took her hand and held it a moment in silence. "Good-bye, my dear friend," he said. "Good luck!" He went to the door and opened it for her.

The tears came into her eyes, but she smiled and, waving her hand to him, left the room.

THE STORM BREAKS IN CREDIN-
TON COURT

CHAPTER XV

THE STORM BREAKS IN CREDINTON COURT

As Rose watched Emily leave the room, she became morally certain that her plan to trap Tom had failed ignominiously. She had no feeling either of pleasure or regret that such should be the case. At the same time she felt that it would be amusing to know the details and to find out whether Tom had suspected the snare that had been set for him.

Freeman came slowly across the room to his book on the window seat and settled himself as if to read.

"Well, Tom," Rose began good-naturedly, "you look quite broken-hearted. Why did you let her go to Australia in this sudden and extraordinary fashion?"

"What could I do about it?" he answered simply.

"Well, if that is the way you feel," she went on, "I don't see why you pull such a long face. You look as if you had vowed never to smile again."

Freeman tossed aside his book. "Doesn't it move you a little," he said sharply, "to see the last of a friend that you've known all your life?"

"I don't think she was ever a very good friend to you," said Rose meaningly. "Besides, she was getting quite impossible, poor thing. People were beginning to fight shy of her."

"Speaking of old friends," said Mr. Peppercorn, "personally I much prefer new acquaintances."

Rose laughed. "That is a sentiment to shock Tom!" she said. "You musn't say such things when he's about."

Freeman left the window seat and stood facing Peppercorn and Rose. "My dear," he said soberly, "you have all long ceased to shock me. I might as well be shocked by the marionettes in a child's theatre."

THE STORM BREAKS

"Hello!" exclaimed Mr. Peppercorn. "What new wheeze is this?"

"At first, when I came home," Freeman went on, ignoring the interruption, "I was frankly horrified. I thought I'd fallen into a perfect sink of iniquity."

"How absurd!" exclaimed Rose.

"How flattering!" corrected Mr. Peppercorn.

"It took me some time to discover," said Freeman, "that you weren't real people at all. You are not men and women, but strange, sexless creatures without blood in your veins, and when one puts you face to face with life," he paused and shrugged his shoulders contemptuously, "you're like a parcel of young ladies painting the Alps in water colours. You can't be wicked. You're too trifling. Your only vice is cigarette smoking, your only passion is bridge. You want nothing very much except to be amused and boredom eats into your very bones. In yourselves you're perfectly unimportant, but England is full of people as frivolous, as flippant and inane. The enemy is at our gates and we're frittering away our time over the games of the circus."

Mr. Peppercorn produced his watch and consulted it with a great deal of manner. "It's lucky I haven't a train to catch," he observed.

"My dear Tom," began Rose with emphasis, "if this outburst of yours is drawn out by my remarks about Emily Chapman, it is just as well that you understand what you are talking about. Emily Chapman cares as little for me as I do for her. It's absurd of you to lecture me like a school girl because I don't have an attack of hysterics when she tells me she is going to Australia."

"As you please," said Freeman quietly.

"I say," said Mr. Peppercorn, perking up, "I wonder why the deuce she's going?"

Rose smiled mischievously. "I should think Tom could tell you more about that than anybody else," she answered.

"Why?" demanded Freeman.

THE STORM BREAKS

"Well," said Rose, "because I fancy she failed in inducing you to marry her and she thought that you were her last chance."

"It may interest you to know that I asked her to marry me," Freeman replied.

"Oh, what fun!" exclaimed Mr. Peppercorn. "What did she say?"

"She refused me," said Freeman.

"Nonsense!" said Rose.

"But the truth," he replied. "And, as you seem to be interested in my matrimonial affairs, I may as well tell you that after she refused me I promptly offered my heart and hand to Smith—"

"What are you talking about?" exclaimed Rose.

"But she," Freeman continued, "strange as it may seem, refused me, too. So now you know *all*, as they say in the play."

Mr. Peppercorn burst into a fit of discordant laughter. "What a joke!" he cried.

"You don't seriously mean to tell me that you asked a servant to marry you?" Rose demanded.

"I did, indeed," said Freeman.

"You must be off your head," his sister replied.

"I think she would make an admirable wife," Freeman went on gravely. "She's the only woman I've seen since I came back who seems capable of being a good housekeeper and a decent mother. She's very simple and she has a good heart, and she's honest and straightforward."

Rose looked at him with mixed incredulity and scorn. "Why did she refuse you?" she asked.

"I'm afraid she didn't think me good enough," he answered.

"It must have been rather a sell for you," observed Mr. Peppercorn.

"It was rather," assented Freeman.

"Tom," demanded Rose, "is this the truth?"

"The whole truth and nothing but the truth," he replied.

She walked stiffly to the bell that was set in the wall by the fireplace and pressed it.

THE STORM BREAKS

"What are you ringing for?" he demanded.

She turned on him haughtily. "Surely," she said, "I can ring the bell in my own house without accounting to you for it."

Freeman went toward her pleadingly. "You're not going to do anything beastly, Rose?" he said.

"I am going to do what I see fit," she replied, "to maintain the dignity, if not the decency of my household." As she finished, the door opened and Smith came in. Rose turned upon her at once. "Smith," she said coldly, "I wish you to leave to-morrow morning."

The girl caught her breath and looked about her in amazement. "Me, ma'am?" she faltered.

"Rose!" exclaimed Freeman indignantly.

"Please leave me alone," she said sharply. "I shall give you a month's money," she went on to Smith, "but I wish you to go to-morrow."

"But what have I done, ma'am, that you don't like?" the girl said meekly.

"I have no explanations to offer," Rose replied. "I shall expect you to be ready at ten o'clock."

"Rose!" exclaimed Freeman, in an undertone, "you can't be such a beast!"

She turned on him angrily, her face white with passion. "Surely I can dismiss my own servants, if I wish to!" she exclaimed.

Smith turned to go without speaking. A stifled sob escaped her, and she left the room.

Brother and sister faced one another for a moment in silence. "How can you be so cruel?" he said at last.

"Don't be absurd," she snapped back. "How can you expect me to keep a servant that you have been making love to? It's too disgraceful! Every tenant in the mansions knows by now that you've asked her to marry you. If you wanted to play this sort of trick, you ought not to have come here. You've made me the laughingstock of the whole place."

"How have I made you the laughingstock of the whole place?" he demanded.

"By your ridiculous conduct," she replied—"by proposing to my parlour maid, the day you say another woman refused you, as if getting a wife was like picking out a set of china."

"Then I may as well tell you," he said soberly, "that it is not like picking out a set of china as far as this woman is concerned. I am just sick with love for her."

"Oh!" cried Rose furiously, "what stuff!"

"I told you that I wanted her for this or that quality," Freeman went on, "but it's all rot. I want her because she is her self and I am my self, because my whole being cries out for her. If this means love,—because I love her—" He paused, changed his tone, and went on again: "You've hated me, Rose, and thought me interfering. I daresay I have been arrogant. If you have felt bitter towards me, you can be satisfied now. You have had revenge enough." He turned on his heel and went out.

Rose heard him going to his room, but made no attempt to call him back. "He is too absurd!" she said.

CHAPTER XVI

MR. PEPPERCORN MAKES AN ANNOUNCEMENT

MR. PEPPERCORN threw his half-smoked cigarette into the fireplace, rose and pulled his coat down, smoothed and buttoned it. "All this emotion is really making me very uncomfortable," he said. "I think I'll be toddling."

Rose looked at him in surprise. "Aren't you lunching here?" she asked.

"I'm afraid I can't," he said uneasily. "Didn't you know?"

"I didn't," said Rose grimly.

"How stupid of mother!" explained Mr. Peppercorn. "I told her to ring you up this morning and tell you."

"She didn't," said Rose. "Where are you lunching?"

"I?" he answered. "Oh, with Lady Whitstable."

"Lady Whitstable is out of town," said Rose. "I saw in the paper this morning that she'd got a week-end party on the river."

"Has she?" exclaimed Mr. Peppercorn with interest. "That's awkward, isn't it?"

"You've rather put your foot in it," said Rose dangerously, "haven't you?"

"I have," said Mr. Peppercorn, with a kind of vague, impersonal regret at the error which had been made. "It shows the danger of snobbishness. If I had said I was lunching with Mrs. Jones or Robinson, you would have been none the wiser."

Rose looked at him searchingly. "Sit down," she said. "What are you hiding from me?"

"I?" said Mr. Peppercorn blandly.

"Oh, don't pretend to be stupider than you are," she insisted. "I know you're hiding something from me. Something is the matter, and I want to know. Why did you tell me that lie?"

"It was stupid of me," said Mr. Peppercorn frankly. "I am lunching with some Americans called Trevor."

"I've never heard of them," said Rose thoughtfully.

"Notwithstanding they have managed to exist," he replied with his old impertinence, "and even to amass a considerable fortune."

She looked at him sharply. "What do you mean?" she demanded.

"I suppose you have guessed it," he said. "If you want to know, I am proposing to marry their young and lovely daughter."

"Are you engaged to her?" Rose asked quickly.

Mr. Peppercorn smiled amiably. "I am," he said.

There was a pause, then Rose spoke again. "How long has this been going on?" she demanded.

"I offered her my young affections at a dance the night before last," he replied. "That would make it forty-eight hours this evening."

"Why haven't you told me anything about

it?" she asked. "You knew that I would be interested."

"Well," said Mr. Peppercorn, "the Trevors are making a little tour around Europe this summer and won't return to London until the late autumn. I thought that there was no need to trouble you about my private affairs until then."

"I suppose," said Rose icily, "that you thought we mightn't be so ready to take you motoring with us this summer if—" She stopped, choked with indignation.

"If what?" inquired Mr. Peppercorn blandly.

"Do you never tell the truth?" she exclaimed.

"Seldom to women," he replied quietly. "I'm always afraid they'll look upon it as an impertinence."

Rose made no reply. Angry as she was, her curiosity about the Trevor girl was paramount. "Is this girl rich?" she asked.

"On the contrary," he answered, "for an American she's very poor. She has barely ten thousand dollars a year, poor thing. We shall have to be rigidly economical. Isn't it a pity, when I so appreciate comfort?"

"Oh, don't laugh all the time!" Rose cried explosively. She threw herself into the armchair by the fire and gazed sullenly at the blazing coals.

"Upon my word, you know!" said Mr. Peppercorn, "I don't see why you're taking it like this! Not a sentiment of congratulation or praise have you expressed."

She turned angrily upon him. "How could you let me go on making all sorts of plans for the future?" she exclaimed. "If you'd had any decent feelings at all, you wouldn't have made such a fool of me!"

"My dear Rose," said Mr. Peppercorn propitiatingly, "women are very peculiar. We got on extremely well together, but you were just as little in love with me as I was with you. It would have bored you, if I had made love to you, just as it would have bored me to do it. But I knew quite well that you didn't want me to make love to anyone else. You liked to think of me as your property and you were looking forward to the pleasure of giving me the chuck when you grew sick of me."

Rose turned her head away. "There's not a soul in the world that cares for me!" she blurted out through angry sobs.

"My dear Rose," Mr. Peppercorn began. He put his hand on her shoulder, but she flung it off with an impatient shrug. He put the spurned member into his trousers pocket and went on, "You are just about to do a very foolish thing. Now that I'm engaged to somebody else, you are going to persuade yourself that you're in love with me."

"How can you have the heart to sneer at me?" she sobbed.

"I'm not sneering at you," he replied. "I'm only suggesting the exercise of a little common sense." He stopped and consulted his watch again. "I really am afraid

AN ANNOUNCEMENT

I must be toddling," he said. "I suppose you'll be in to supper?" he added.

Rose shot him a look of loathing. "No," she said. She dried her eyes, got up and went to the piano.

"That is a nuisance," he said calmly. "I shall have to sup with mother. Still, what can't be cured, you know—"

Rose took a cigarette from a silver box on the piano top and nervously lit it. "You need not give yourself the trouble of coming here again," she said. "I have come to the conclusion that you bore me."

"Just as you like," Mr. Peppercorn replied calmly. "But you see, now, how wise I was to keep the happy news of my engagement locked in my own manly bosom?"

"You'll be too late for your party," said Rose satirically.

Mr. Peppercorn smiled good-naturedly. "Good-bye," he said. "I'm sure you'll like my wife." He held out his hand, but she drew away with a shudder of disgust.

"You cad!" she exclaimed.

Mr. Peppercorn laughed lightly. "Well, good-bye again," he said, and went out.

A few moments later Freeman re-entered the drawing-room and found Rose on the couch, her face buried in a cushion.

"Hello," he said, "what's the matter? I thought I heard Algy go out."

She lifted her head and looked at him bitterly. "He's gone for good," she said.

"Has he?" said Freeman calmly. "Well, I don't think he's much loss."

"What have I done?" she went on slowly. "Emily's gone and Cynthia won't see me, and now he's gone, too. Why have they all left me at once? I might be plague-stricken."

"I think they left you," said Freeman in a kindly tone, "because you never tried to make them your friends. You used them for your pleasure, as they used you for theirs. It's very hard to make friends. It requires that one should give all oneself without a thought of return. But you might find it worth while."

"I despise them all!" cried Rose, leaping to her feet. "They're beneath contempt!"

"Steady!" said Freeman gently. "Perhaps it isn't their fault altogether. You've got precious little out of life so far. Why don't you try a change? You've got a chance that you'll never have again."

Rose looked at him, and for a moment her lip quivered and she hesitated. "Can the Ethiopian change his skin or the leopard his spots?" she said slowly. "I'm not made like you, Tom. No," she continued, speaking more rapidly, "no, I must go on as I've begun. If a few acquaintances have left me, I can make more. I'm not going to worry my head about them. There are as good fish in the sea as ever were caught." She went nervously to the door and began to call her husband. He gave her an answering "Hello!" from his study. "Be quick, I want you!" she called. She came restlessly back into the room, took her hat from the table and began putting it on with feverish haste.

A moment later Dallas-Baker put his head in. "Yes, my dear," he said. "What's the matter?"

"Be quick!" she exclaimed. "Get into your coat, I want you! Let's go and lunch at Princes's, you and I. We can't lunch in. There's been a catastrophe in the kitchen."

Dallas-Baker looked at her perplexed. "Why, Rose, what's the matter with you?" he asked.

She laughed hysterically. "Nothing's the matter with me," she answered. "But I'm bored. I want gaiety. I want the crowd, and the band, and the noise!"

"Just as you like, my dear," her husband replied. "But what about Tom?"

"That's arranged," said Freeman quickly. "I'm going to my club."

"Very well," said Dallas-Baker doubtfully. "I'll change my coat."

"Hurry!" Rose called after him. "It's awfully late." She turned to her brother, but spoke as if to herself or to some impersonal auditor. "I won't be bored!" she said passionately. "I'm going to amuse myself. I want the crowd, and the band, and the gaiety! And afterwards we'll take a taxi and go down to Ranlegh."

Freeman watched her, hoping for an opportunity to speak, but she gave him none. He went to her and laid his hand soothingly on her arm, but she flung him off and paced restlessly to and fro the length of the room, swallowing the sobbing that choked her.

Presently her husband returned. "I'm ready, dear," he said.

"Then hurry," she answered and, dabbing at her eyes with a handkerchief, she led the way out.

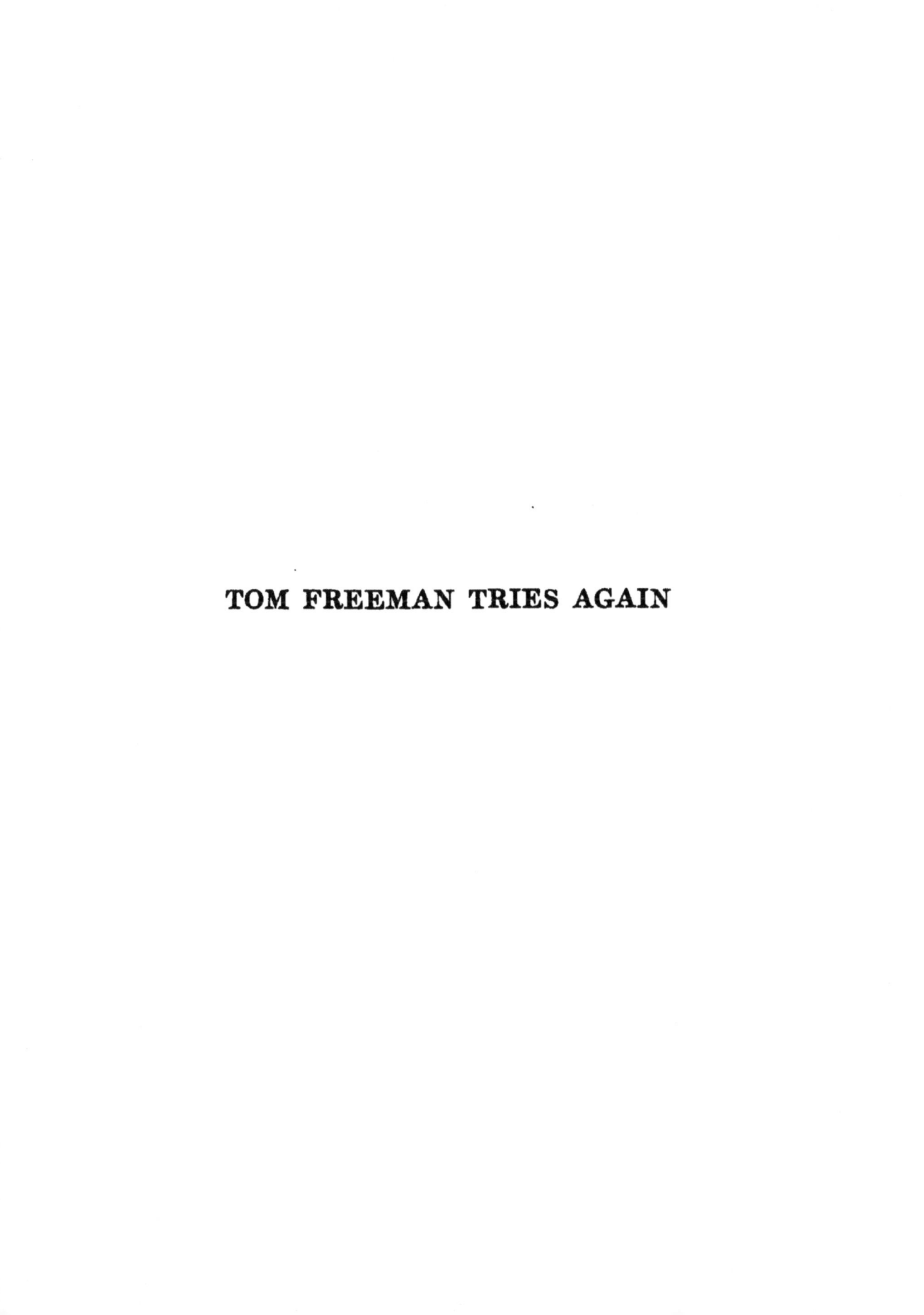

TOM FREEMAN TRIES AGAIN

CHAPTER XVII

TOM FREEMAN TRIES AGAIN

FREEMAN stood in the middle of the room, blankly wondering at the scene to which he had been witness, till he heard the front door close with a bang. Then he shook his head sorrowfully and went to the armchair by the fire, sat down and mechanically sought the solace of tobacco. He smoked for perhaps three minutes, considering the situation in which he found himself. Rose had passed out of his life. Emily Chapman was off for Australia, and he was on the eve of sailing back to South Africa again. The only living creature that he regretted leaving was Smith. Smith and her problem and the complications which he had unwittingly introduced into it laid very heavily on his heart. The worst of it was that he seemed powerless to do anything. "One can't adopt a beautiful parlour maid," he murmured. Assistance of a financial nature, he knew that she would not accept, yet he had caused her dismissal and was morally responsible in a way for making it up to her. But over and beyond that, as he had confessed to Rose, he was in love with her, which, as she did not return the sentiment, only tended further to complicate matters.

However, Freeman had never been the kind of man that withers in inaction. He had made many mistakes, but never that of doing nothing. Just as it seemed to him that there was nothing to do except to slip off to Rhodesia by the next ship, a smile came to his lips. He tossed his cigarette into the fireplace, rose, took a vase of flowers from the mantelpiece, went to the window, poured out part of the water and then, coming back to the centre table, strewed them and the rest of the water on the floor, laying the vase on its side, as if it had accidentally been knocked from the table. After surveying his work with some satisfaction, he went to the bell and rang. Then he lighted another cigarette and sat down.

After a suitable interval, Smith appeared. She carried herself even straighter and with more dignity than was usual, and her eyes looked red and swollen. "Did you ring, sir?" she asked.

"Yes," he answered disingenuously. "It was very stupid of me. I knocked a flower glass off the table. I wonder if you would bring me a duster?"

"Yes, sir," she said. She went to one of the bookcases, opened a drawer in the bottom and came back with a dust cloth.

"Thank you," he said, and came forward as if to take it.

"Oh, no; I'll do it," she said firmly. She got down on her knees and began to wipe up the carpet and gather the flowers back into the vase.

"It's lucky it wasn't broken, isn't it?" he suggested.

"Yes, sir," she answered. Her voice had

a little break in it and he noticed that, as she bent her head over her work, twice she put her hand to her eyes.

"You've been crying," he said gently.

"No, I haven't, sir," she answered sharply, but without looking up at him.

"I apologise then," he said. "Do you mind my asking if you are much put out at leaving?"

"No one has ever given me notice before, sir," she said miserably. "I don't like being spoken to like a dog."

"I'm very sorry about that," he said gravely. "It's all my fault. It never occurred to me that my sister could take it in that way."

"Oh, it doesn't matter," she answered. "Cook said it was bound to come!"

"Cook seems to be a confirmed pessimist," he observed.

"It won't take me long to find another place," she went on. She finished gathering up the flowers and, rising, placed them on the table again.

"I thought you were going to your sister's at Sydney," he said.

Smith shook her head. "I can't do that now, sir," she replied. "I had a letter from her last week, saying that she and her husband were coming home for a holiday."

"Oh!" said Freeman. "Then perhaps you'd like to stay on here. My sister speaks very sharply on the impulse, but I daresay she would—"

Smith interrupted him with quiet dignity. "Thank you very much, sir," she said, "but I shouldn't like to stay in a place where I'd been given notice for no fault of my own."

"Have your own way," he answered, "but I call it sinful pride."

"I call it a proper spirit," she answered firmly.

He looked at her questioningly. "Then," said he, "it seems to me that the only thing that remains is Fletcher."

"Thank you, it will be a long time before I marry Fletcher!" she replied with spirit. As she spoke about Fletcher, she seemed either to forget or lay aside the professional Smith more than she had ever done before in his presence, and to his eyes her beauty and charm increased accordingly.

"What has Fletcher done?" he asked.

"I made up my mind and told him I wouldn't, that's all," she explained.

"Why did you do that?" he demanded.

Smith smiled in spite of herself. "You remember that cork that you drew?" she asked.

"Of course I do," he answered. "The young Hercules couldn't manage it, could he?"

"Well," continued Smith, "I told him that if he couldn't draw a cork that a gentleman could draw, he must be a weak little thing. I was only chaffing him, sir, but he got quite nasty about it, and one thing led to another, and at last, to make a long story short, I told him he could take himself off," and she added simply: "Last Wednesday he went out with the girl upstairs."

"It seems to me," Freeman observed

gravely, "that you are rather at a loose end."

She made no reply, for her eyes were fixed on the flowers on the table and she seemed to be working out something in her mind. "Excuse me, sir," she said with some hesitation.

"What's the matter?" he asked.

"Well, sir," she went on, "how did you knock these flowers off the *table* when I distinctly remember putting them on the mantelpiece?"

"I didn't knock them off the table," he answered solemnly. "I put them very carefully on the floor, so that you should have the bother of clearing them up."

Smith looked at him in hopeless perplexity, then a smile broke on her lips, and next she laughed. "You are a caution!" she exclaimed in her low, delightful voice.

Freeman took a step forward and squared his shoulders. "Why don't you change your mind and marry me?" he asked. He attempted to carry it off gaily, but his voice trembled.

"Thank you very much, sir," she said decidedly, "but when I say *no*, I mean *no*."

"Have you any objection to me personally?" he asked in desperation.

She smiled again. "No, sir," she answered, "I can't say that I have."

They were silent for a moment, gazing at one another, then he began, his voice uncertain with emotion. "You know at first," he said, "I asked you to marry me because I wanted a wife. Now I ask you to marry me because I want *you*."

As he finished, the duster slipped from her hand, her lips began to quiver, and suddenly, like a child, she burst into tears and, dropping into the armchair by the fire, she hid her face in her hands.

"What the devil is the matter, now?" he exclaimed.

"Why couldn't you leave me alone?" she sobbed.

"Oh, my dear, don't! don't!" he said protestingly.

"I was quite happy till you came," she

went on brokenly. "I've never done you any harm and you—" She stopped, unable to go on and gave herself up to sobbing.

The colour left Freeman's face and his voice trembled. "Is it possible that you care?" he said. "For God's sake, don't play the fool with me now!" He took her hands and drew them gently away from her face.

"If you really cared for me," she said sorrowfully, "you wouldn't have proposed as if it was a joke." She snatched her hands away. "I hate you!" she exclaimed fiercely. "I've always tried to do my best, and you come here and—" she began to choke again—"I haven't deserved it," she sobbed.

"Oh, my dear," he said earnestly, "if you only knew how much I loved you! It would make me so desperately happy, if I thought you could ever care for me!"

"Cook was quite right," she said, as if speaking to herself; "I ought to have gone at once."

"Oh, damn cook!" he exclaimed impatiently.

"I didn't know it was coming over me like this," she went on. "I never gave you a thought till you asked me, and then—and then," she added simply, "I thought I'd liked you ever since you came." She dropped back into the chair from which she had risen, and he took her hands and knelt beside her.

"Oh, my darling," he said, "do you mean it?"

She made no reply, but dropped her head on his shoulder. Her cap became disarranged, and she put up a hand to replace it.

"Take the damned thing off!" he cried.

With a swift movement she unpinned it and smiled at him.

"Good Lord!" he exclaimed. "I didn't know you had such hair!"

She said nothing, but sat there, gazing at him with misty eyes, her little head crowned with a glory of straw-coloured hair.

He rose slowly and drew her to her feet.

"My dear," he said, and put his arm about her, but she drew away again.

"Oh, don't!" she said pitifully. "It wouldn't do. Just think of the difference. I'm not good enough for you."

"Bosh!" he cried savagely. "Now tell me what your name is."

She laughed and hid her face on his shoulder. "Mary," she whispered.

"How ripping!" he exclaimed. "That's just what I wanted it to be!"

THE END